GREED

FRANCESCO VEZZOLI

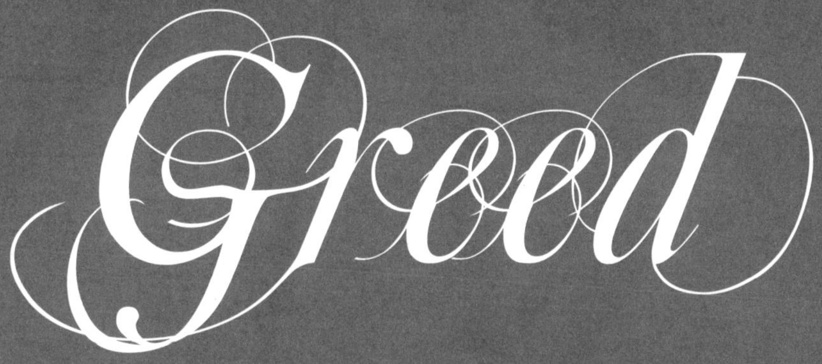

Greed

LA CONSERVERA

Verlag der Buchhandlung Walther König

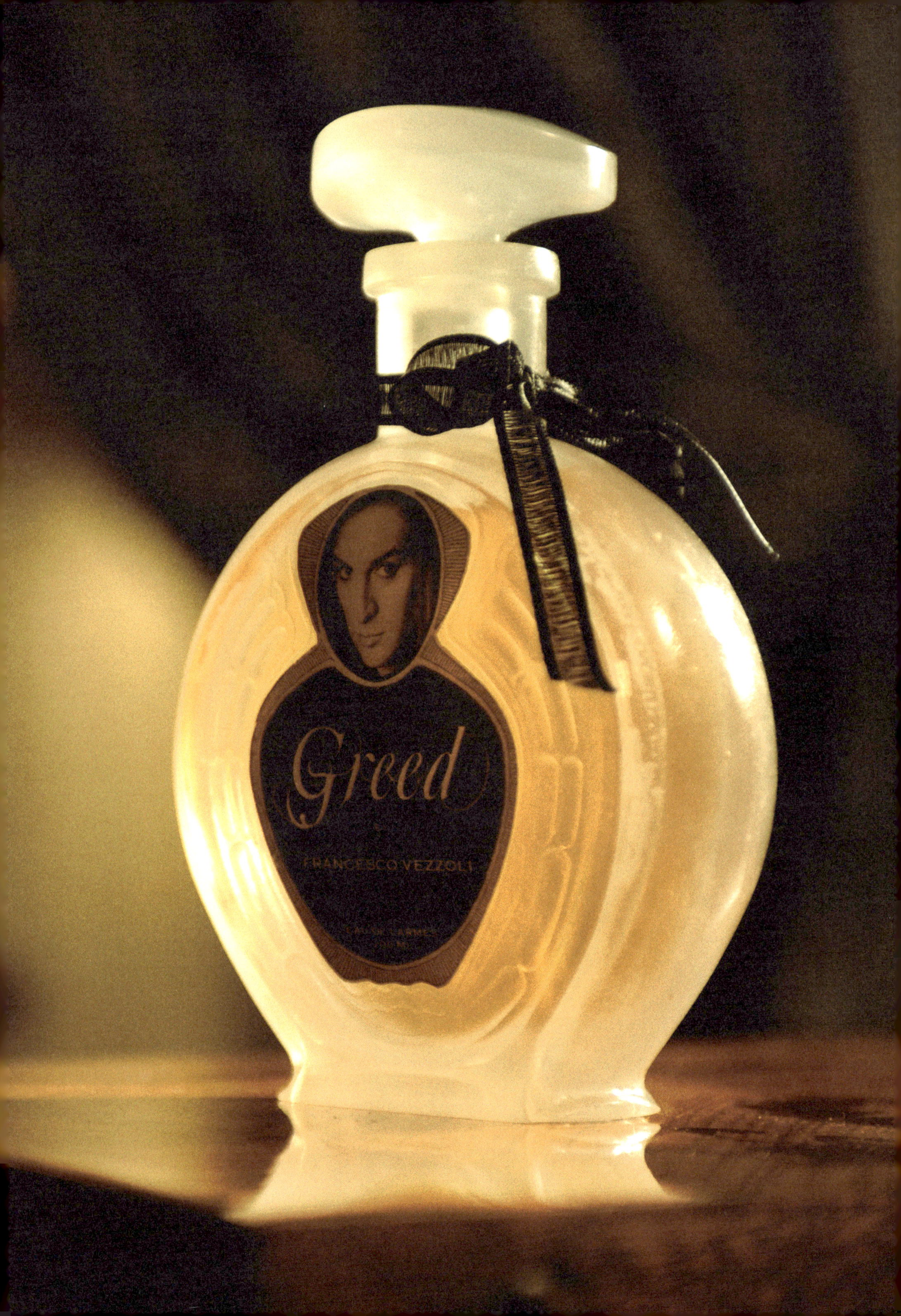
Greed
FRANCESCO VEZZOLI

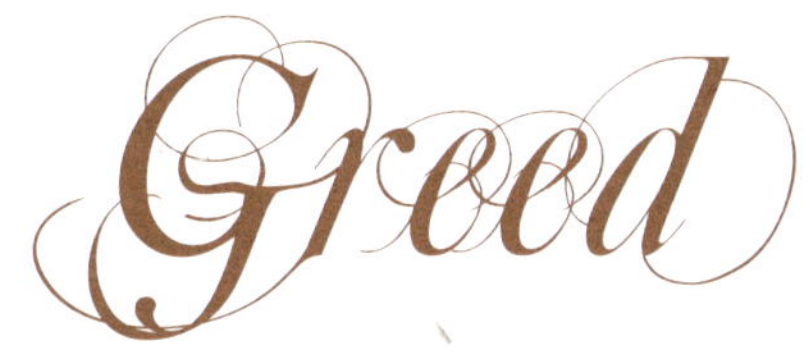

The Law of Desire
By Cristiana Perrella

Protect me from what I want
Jenny Holzer

March 2009. In Paris, against the unique backdrop of the Gran Palais, what would later be called "the auction of the century" put on the block the incalculable, eclectic collection of modern masterpieces and antique furniture, Art Deco pieces and 19th-century paintings, works of silver, ivory and porcelain gathered over a span of fifty years by Yves Saint Laurent and his companion and partner Pierre Bergé. When the French couturier passed away, Bergé decided to sell everything in order to donate the proceeds (a record: 373.9 million euros) to the fight against AIDS. Among the over 700 lots in the auction there was the *Belle Haleine, Eau de Voilette* by Marcel Duchamp, an assisted readymade done in 1921 in New York with the help of Man Ray: a bottle of *Un Air Embaumé*, the famous perfume of the *maison* Rigaud, "personalized" by replacing the original label with another in which the word game appears that gives the work its title, and a portrait of the artist in drag, posing as Rrose Sélavy, his feminine alter ego. This work was sold to an as yet unidentified bidder for 8.9 million euros.

Francesco Vezzoli could not have imagined that the *Belle Haleine* would become the most desired and costly perfume bottle of all time when he decided to construct around it, for an exhibition at Gagosian in Rome that opened one month prior to the famous auction, a project he had had in mind for some time[1]: a fake advertising campaign for the launch of a non-existent fragrance, *Greed*.

Yet this latest chapter of the history of one of the rare surviving original Duchamp's readymades[2] seems to have been written just for him. Fashion, glamour, sophisticated taste and melancholy for the end of a great gay love story are connected with the unchallenged intellectual status of a conceptual masterpiece, that then winds up being vied for, to the tune of millions, by the nouveaux riches in the spotlight of the "auction of the century": the work by Duchamp becomes the most "Vezzolian" citation imaginable, especially with respect to one of the primary ways of working of the Italian artist. Namely that of putting to the test, through contamination with commercial, unbecoming, melodramatic elements, the intellectual respectability and validity of the rooted system of references that forms the foundation of the art world, in an era in which that world, and society as a whole, are obsessed with and changed by the dynamics of the star system, the spectacular, the primacy of the market.

Can we still imagine an aspect of art that eludes these mechanisms? Can we believe that art's historical and philosophical role can remain unscathed?

Vezzoli answers these questions by remaking Dorian Gray with Veruschka (*Veruschka Was Here*, 2001), by transforming Pasolini into a reality show (*Non Love Meetings*, 2004), by staging an American presidential campaign with Bernard-Henry Levi and Sharon Stone as the candidates (*Democrazy*, 2007), by putting the Bolshoi together with Lady Gaga (*Ballets Russes Italian Style [The Shortest Musical You Will Never See Again]*, 2009). Or by filling the wall of a museum with portraits of famous stars, their faces striped by embroidered Lurex tears, or translating the rigorous geometric Bauhaus designs of Joseph Albers into little domestic needlepoint panels.

The complex question of how art fits into the postindustrial world is approached without simplification by Vezzoli, who refuses to resolve it in the antithesis of opposition to or celebration of the status quo, and instead takes a much more articulate position, and thus one that is often accused of ambiguity.

But this ambiguity, this being in the middle, confusing the order, the rules, the confines, this abjection –as David Rimanelli correctly calls it, citing Julia Kristeva[3]- is precisely the crucial feature of Vezzoli's work. Work through which the artist, assuming the problematic position of art infatuated with the media, with economic and social power, reveals –as with a magnifying mirror- its excesses and contradictions, demonstrating (but without detachment, without moralism, even shouldering the risks of the situation himself) how the borderline between what is acceptable and what is not has become irreparably fluid.

"I like the decadent, corrupt aspect of things –he says. – We live in a society that condemns you in terms of media, lumping you together with what you don't like; we are in an intellectual moment where it is impossible to preserve the integrity of your work. So if you cannot keep your *hortus* clean, the weapon is sarcastic contamination of the most absurdly contrasting values"[4].

A careful connoisseur of the codes of the "society of the spectacle", Vezzoli takes possession of them and uses them as tools to propose, under a sparkling surface, a daring mixture of tradition and radicalism, televised trash and erudite references, *Hollywood Babylon* and incursions into art history, politics and personal obsessions, without fearing the transformation of the serious into the frivolous, aesthetization, taste for excess, the scandal of the contamination of forms and meanings, often ignited by surreal plots

–videos or performances- that include the participation (free of charge) of increasingly stellar celebrities. "I like to think that I'm corrupting different audiences –he says in another interview. – Everybody who 'buys' my Helmut Berger has to 'buy' the other obscure references. And everybody who 'buys' the intellectual depth has to 'buy' into my fetishes"[5].

But Vezzoli doesn't just corrupt. He also, above all, seduces. He seduces stars to convince them to take part in his projects, he seduces the backers that make the projects possible, he seduces the audience, always conceding entertainment elements that catch one's interest and lead toward the denser, more profound parts of his works. Not just deployed but thematically pertinent, seduction is a ubiquitous feature of his work. Seduction and its motor, desire, starting with his first efforts, like the needlepoint reproductions of postcards with offers of sex by payment found in London telephone booths –the artist was a student in that city in the early 1990s– or the embroidered portrait of Jeff Stryker, the openly gay porno star.

The matrix of a substantially auto-erotic, narcissistic sexuality like that of the present day, the desire is not instinct, is not based on biological necessities of reproduction; it is a pure mental construct, an impulse fulfilled above all by itself, enticed more by its desiring activity than by any finally achieved relationship with its object. As Lacan says, it is transversal jouissance.

Organized, cultivated, manipulated, desire probably has a cultural relevance today it has never had in any other historical period. Not because the needs are stronger – far from it. It is because the increase in the quantity and intensity of desires is the raw material of an economics that collapses if it does not grow, making development into an imperative. Desire is the main ingredient of the narrations and dreams that sustain the industry of consumption and political consensus. It is the primary product of advertising and cinema.

Art too, in the postindustrial phase, participates in this "strategy of desire", contributing to a true redefinition of the conceptual nature of products, of their way of being with respect to consumers. The conquest of increasingly wide popularity on the part of artists, often true celebrities today, combined with the status of uniqueness and unaffordability of their works for mass consumption (reinforced by constantly rising prices), give art what the economist Pier Luigi Sacco calls a "post-Benjamin aura"[6] that becomes an essential ingredient in the perception of the value of an object, whenever the association is made, nurturing a perfect machine of desire. The case

of the collaboration of Takashi Murakami with Vuitton, in this case, is
emblematic.

Precisely this point of convergence where art aspires to achieve the power of
the media, while the media seek the aura of art to achieve better sales, is the
location of *Greed. A New Fragrance By Francesco Vezzoli*. Between imaginary
and desire, abjection and seduction.

Aping the strategy and aesthetic of a campaign to launch a new fragrance,
Vezzoli transforms the space of the gallery or museum (Gagosian in Rome in
2009, then in 2011 La Conservera, in Murcia) into a luxurious boutique, walls
covered in red velvet, a sort of "cross between a boudoir and a funeral parlor",
as a journalist salaciously commented on the "society pages" of Artforum.
com[7]. At the center, in a glass display case, looms a magnum bottle of the
perfume, a *monstre* version of Duchamp's *Belle Haleine*, with Vezzoli dressed
in feminine clothes on the label, in a shot by Francesco Scavullo –the glamour
eye of Warhol's *Interview*- in place of Rrose Sélavy. The name of the perfume
is *Greed, Eau de larmes*, in a multiple reference to what has emerged, after the
crisis of Wall Street, as the most contemporary of the deadly sins, to the lost
film maudit of the same name by the great Eric von Stroheim[8] –a director who
hated the star system- and to the tears that streak the faces of Vezzoli's most
iconic embroideries.

And tears of pearls, rhinestones, Lurex or black thread spurt from the eyes
of the women artists used as testimonials on big embroidered canvases,
precious damasks printed with a Magritte-like sky background, hung
on the walls like promotional posters. Georgia O'Keeffe, with her severe
visage forged by the winds of New Mexico, Lee Miller, gorgeous, a model
for Vogue in the 1920s, Frida Kahlo, iconic, then Eva Hesse and Tamara De
Lempicka, Tina Modotti and Leonor Fini, Meret Oppenheim, Niki de Saint
Phalle, Sonia Delaunay, Louise Nevelson, perversely chosen to combine
figures of irreprehensible artistic reputation with others that are hopelessly
commercial. A parade of stars (who else?) of 20th-century art, whose talent
–often overshadowed and a bit exploited by a lover or husband who was also
an artist- has not always met with the acclaim it deserved. Their suffering, as
women, brings them closer to the other *Crying Divas* immortalized by Vezzoli.

Divas to the utmost, so divine they have never gotten entangled with
advertising (at least not until Vezzoli came along to convince them), are
Natalie Portman and Michelle Williams, actresses chosen by the artist
to make a television ad just one minute in length (which will never be
aired), directed by Roman Polanski. The director of *Rosemary's Baby* draws

inspiration from *Les Vampires*, a French serial from 1915 by Louis Feuillade and a cult item for the Surrealists, assigning Williams a role reminding of Irma Vep –with a black Prada hood- and with his typical dark, cynical sense of humor he transforms the glamorous, glossy atmosphere of a fashion ad over the notes of Chopin into the farce of a mad struggle, no holds barred, between the two women for possession of the precious perfume. In the heat of the battle the bottle would surely be smashed, were it not for the artist himself, who intervenes to rescue it. The close-up of his foot in splendid black patent leather is one of the final frames.

Once again, like a wild impresario, or in this case a brilliant *mad man*, but too sophisticated to be understood by consumers, Vezzoli stages an over the top, overproduced show and weaves, under the surface of an attractive, apparently facile idea, a labyrinthine plot of references, just the opposite of the brutal simplification found in the media language he apes in his work. As in a Borgesian game of mirrors, he starts with Duchamp who brings a commercial object into the space of art, changing its status, then takes the work that is the result of this *detournement* and treats it as if it were merchandise to promote, using art (the artist-testimonials, Polanski) to sell it better. But alas this campaign, orchestrated so perfectly that an advertisement also appeared in the *Herald Tribune* on the day of the opening, is based on nothing, a fragrance that doesn't exist, replaced in the big crystal bottle by five liters of bourbon, an old trick worthy of the dressing room of a movie star headed for her own sunset boulevard. After having done a pilot for a reality dating show that will never be broadcast (*Non-Love Meetings*, 2004), a trailer for a film that doesn't exist (*Trailer for a Remake of Gore Vidal's Caligula*, 2005), an election campaign for two fake candidates (*Democrazy*, 2007), rehearsals for a play that will never make its debut (*Right You Are If You Think You Are*, 2007), for Vezzoli building on the void, on absence, on unkept promise, is something of a habit. Or more precisely, it is his strategy of deconstruction of the "law of desire", to lay bare the functioning of the mechanism of continuous, widespread seduction deployed by the media, which is the motor of our era, constantly reminding us of an original lack, a void of meaning no merchandise can ever fill.

1   In an interview with Germano Celant in 2004, he hints at "[…] something like putting a perfume bottle in an exhibition in such a way that people understand it is not a real perfume bottle, a bit like the perfume bottle of Duchamp. For me this is the finest perversion", in Germano Celant, *Francesco Vezzoli*, Fondazione Prada, Progetto Prada Arte, Milano, 2004, p.129

2   Most of the readymades of Duchamp were destroyed after they were exhibited. In 1964, however, Duchamp commissioned Arturo Schwarz to make multiple replicas of the most important ones, which were done in Milan. Their production for commercial ends surprised the friends and fans of Duchamp. Max Ernst even commented that "the value of the gesture that had ensured the great beauty of the readymade" had been forever compromised. Unlike the other original works, the *Belle Haleine* was not destroyed because Duchamp had given it to his lover at the time, Yvonne Crotti.

3   "At the risk of being very pretentious – any serious discussion of Vezzoli's work seems to entail a certain risk, so whatever- I would align his project with the theoretical debates swirling around abjection. 'It is thus not lack of cleanliness or health that causes abjection but what disturbs identity, system, order' Julia Kristeva writes. 'What does not respect borders, positions, rules. The in-between, the ambiguous, the composite'" in David Rimanelli, "The Best Defence Is a Good Offence", in Francesco *Vezzoli: A True Hollywood Story!*, The Power Plan, Toronto, 2008, p. 23.

4   G. Celant, op. cit. p 255

5   Interview conducted by Barbara Steiner in Jan Winkelmann (ed.), *The Needleworks of Francesco Vezzoli*, Hatje Kantz, Ostfildern, 2003, p.12

6   Pier Luigi Sacco, "Oltre lo sboom: le correnti sotterranee dell'arte contemporanea" in Adriana Polveroni, *Lo sboom. Il decennio dell'arte pazza tra bolla finanziaria e flop concettuale*, Silvana editoriale, Milano, 2009, p. 100.

7   Cathryn Drake, *Rrose Sélavy's Baby*, in "Scene & Herd", 14 February 2009, Artforum.com

8   Considered one of the key films in cinema history, *Greed* was made by Von Stroheim in 1924. It had a very high budget for the time, but its original version, composed of 42 reels and with a length of about eight hours, was shown only once, in a private screening. The studio shortened the film to two hours using its own editors, rendering the work incomprehensible. Much of the cut material was destroyed.

Socialite Realism
By Nicholas Cullinan

[It] is more than a frivolous work. It is a monument to frivolity!
Jean Cocteau[1]

All style and no substance. This is perhaps the very highest tribute that can be paid to the work of Francesco Vezzoli; a perversely appropriate backhanded compliment for an artist who thrives on inverting everything around him and who is the most eloquent cipher possible for our image-infatuated age. Through Vezzoli's adroit manoeuvres, the Marxian prophesy 'All that is solid melts into air' is made real for the wireless era of the Internet, and a penetrating and many-tentacled satire is constructed through little more than celebrity, glamour and media manipulation. So successful has this operation been that the supposedly 'media-obsessed antics' of Vezzoli were hand-picked (or picked on) as being indicative of both the success and failure of Italian art in the opening sentence of the introduction to a recent special issue of the journal October on post-war Italian art: 'If Francesco Vezzoli's recent star-studded Pirandello extravaganza at the Solomon R. Guggenheim Museum and the *Senso Unico* exhibition that ran concurrently at P.S.1 Contemporary Art Center are any indication, contemporary Italian art has finally arrived.'[2]

Vezzoli, growing up as a star-struck teenager in provincial Brescia, recalls having a poster of a work by Mario Merz on his wall.[3] But it was Alighiero Boetti's tapestries that arguably wove their influence onto Vezzoli, who first came to prominence for his series of embroidered portraits of Hollywood stars with the camp addition of overlaid tears. Vezzoli's subsequent unpicking of episodes in Modernism can be traced back to early works such as irreverent homages to the Bauhaus severity and precision of Josef Albers or the epic Abstract Expressionism of Mark Rothko's canvases, both of which are deflated and scaled down into needlepoint by Vezzoli; or the Futurist Fortunato Depero's designs for magazines such as Vanity Fair and Vogue, which are seized upon and flaunted by Vezzoli in *DiscoDepero* from 2003. Perhaps most scurrilously of all, Vezzoli cast a queer eye over one of the most avowedly heterosexual holy cows of Conceptualism in *The Bruce Nauman Trilogy*, 2005-2006. Vezzoli solicits a queer re-reading of Bruce Nauman's *Bouncing Balls* (1969), by straying salaciously from the territory of rigorous conceptualism to flagrant pornography. Recently, Vezzoli has created mise en scènes for an exhibition of the decidedly sold out works of Salvador Dali and his most outré activities, or reinterpreted Alexander

Rodchenko's Russian Constructivism and designs by Giorgio de Chirico for Sergei Diaghilev's Ballets Russes to act as stage sets and backdrops for Lady Gaga's mushrooming fame (as Vezzoli rightly spots, a prima ballerina for our age if ever there was one). Andy Warhol famously created his own brand of parodic 'Superstars' out of misfits and oddballs, but Vezzoli instead treats celebrity itself as a readymade, co-opting a roll call of the great and good, and, as always, the bigger, the better.

Special guest stars
Aspiration has long been the art world's dirty secret. The thing that none of us, no matter how much we may want, wish to admit to. A desire that dare not drop its name, so to speak. And it is precisely this elaborate masquerade to avoid the uncomfortably arriviste truth that Vezzoli flaunts so shamelessly before us in each of his projects. What do the following phenomena have in common? A pilot for a game show that will never go on air, a breathless trailer for a Hollywood epic that will never be made, glossy electoral propaganda for non-existent candidates, and an overheated premiere of a play that will never run beyond its self-imploding first night. The answer is that these spectacles are all constructed by Vezzoli to adhere so faithfully to the rules of their respective games, that their essential vacuity and inherent failure is at first obscured by the razzle-dazzle that not only attends them, but upon closer inspection is revealed as their only real trace.

Vezzoli's film *Trailer for a Remake of Gore Vidal's 'Caligula'*, (2005) which was shown at both the 2005 Venice Biennale and the Whitney Biennial the following year, brought him to widespread attention and provides a crucial precedent for his subsequent works. An overblown advertisement for a film that that doesn't exist, Vezzoli's *'Caligula'* reheats ancient Roman history as schlock sub-Hollywood entertainment with a political parable for our age. This tactic has been continued by projects such as *MARLENE REDUX: A True Hollywood Story!*, a video project that legitimately managed to conflate the Hollywood star Marlene Dietrich with Bauhaus figure Anni Albers, courtesy of the historical fluke which saw the latter making a fleeting appearance in Maximilian Schell's 1984 documentary Marlene, and Vezzoli's all-star, one-night-only performance of Luigi Pirandello's 1917 play, *Cosi è [se vi pare]*, or, *Right You Are (If You Think You Are)*, at the Solomon R. Guggenheim Museum, New York in 2007. Pirandello's original work explored the small-town gossip of a typical and anonymous Italian village, whose characters speculate on the moral character and private life of an elusive and almost entirely off-stage 'Signora Ponza' (played by

Cate Blanchett). Vezzoli transposed this setting into a modern parable on the obsession with celebrity and fame, writ-large by virtue of the setting, cast and anticipation created around the event.

If Francesco Vezzoli was a movie, Hollywood couldn't afford him. Such is the star power that he is able to co-opt into his lavishly vacuous productions, that even only a partial list would include the likes of Lady Gaga, Courtney Love, Natalie Portman, Sharon Stone, Bianca Jagger, etc, etc… Through this, Vezzoli yokes the current premium placed on collaborative art-making to the exact opposite esteem in which the art world holds such unabashed social climbing and celebrity endorsement.

The Sweet Smell of Success

Vezzoli's recent endeavour ups this ante still further, with a nod back to the readymade of Marcel Duchamp. *Greed, a New Fragrance by Francesco Vezzoli*, takes as its starting point Duchamp's assisted readymade from 1921 *Belle Haleine: Eau de Voilette* (Beautiful Breath, Veil Water) and riffs of his appropriation of a Rigaud perfume bottle adorned with an alternate label of the artist photographed in drag as his alter ego Rrose Sélavy by Man Ray. Vezzoli however, scales up Duchamp's ambition by producing an ostentatiously outsize perfume bottle made of crystal (made in collaboration with Italian artisans, naturally) and plastering this with a photograph of himself in drag by the fashion photographer Francesco Scavullo. Vezzoli also co-opts Roman Polanski to direct an advertisement for the fictitious fragrance staring the Hollywood stars Natalie Portman and Michelle Williams and appropriates a host of other female artists from Eva Hesse to Meret Oppenheim to become unlikely poster girls for his new (and entirely fictitious) product. Like Vezzoli, Duchamp invented his alter ego Rose (later Rrose) Sélavy in 1920 'not to change my identity, but to have two identities.'[4] But unlike Vezzoli's ambivalent cooption of his female counterparts, Duchamp seems to have invented Rrose Sélavy as a cover for his most debased or commercial activities, to pimp her out as it were, and in so doing, put material desire into drag.[5] But set against this supposed cynicism, must be placed the earnest craft and care inherent in the methods of production of Vezzoli's work. For, as he is eager to point out, all the stitches are his own and each object is hand crafted.[6]

'Made in Italy' was also a label scurrilously undermined one of Vezzoli's spiritual ancestors, Piero Manzoni, in a project which is the twin to Vezzoli's perfume, and reeks of nothing as much as cynicism. In 1961, at the height of the miracolo italiano, Piero Manzoni produced ninety cans of *Merda d'artista* (Artist's Shit). Made in Italy, but labelled in several languages for international exportation, the excrement was intended to be sold at the same price, per gramme, as gold. As Manzoni commented upon his man-made products: 'In May '61 I produced and canned 90 boxes of 'artist's shit' (30 gr. each) preserved au naturel (made in Italy)'.[7] Manzoni's 'products' (simultaneously organic and 'man-made') may be viewed as a scatological satire of the *miracolo italiano*, by alchemically turning the base material of shit into that of the most precious – gold, and indexing his work to the fluctuating market value of this commodity.[8] Manzoni's miraculous product, the packaging of which is arguably more important than the still-mysterious product within them, predictably drew harsh criticism.[9] The strategies of artists such as Manzoni and Yves Klein, vex Lucy Lippard's notion of the 'dematerialisation of the art object' in the 1960s as a purist strategy to negate the art market.[10] Instead, these two leading proponents of the monochrome deployed dematerialisation as a form of con-trick and charlatanism through, for example, Klein selling seven identically sized IKB monochrome paintings for different prices at his 1957 solo show at the Galleria Apollinaire in Milan to supposedly reflect imperceptible differences in quality, his empty presentation of the gallery with La Vide in 1958 and Manzoni's credulity-testing *Merda d'artista* and *Base magica* (Magic Base) of 1961.

The label 'made in Italy' is a particularly persistent one, it seems. Vezzoli's satirical remakes, for better or for worse, are proof that Italian art has finally made it. Elaborately constructed around ciphers and voids, and whose glitzy packaging only serves to underscore the emptiness of their contents, Vezzoli therefore continues Klein's and Manzoni's vehement refutation of the taste and politics of the day. Rather, Vezzoli's shape-shifting work, ambitious beyond any boundary, is taken in some accounts as being symptomatic of 'the precise eradication of national and cultural boundaries that is characteristic of today's global media culture.'[11] In a diary entry from the 1980s, as Andy Warhol's critical reputation steadily atrophied, reviled as he was for his brazen embrace of commerce and celebrity, he resignedly wrote on the eve of the opening of one of his exhibitions: 'The reviews will be bad, as they always are, but the reviews of the party will be great.' Vezzoli, whose work is in essence often only the party, is remaking for our own age and in our very image, Andy's superficially shallow disco décor, and we are all invited.

1   Jean Cocteau on his libretto for Diaghilev's Ballets Russes 1924 production *Le Train Bleu*.

2   Claire Gilman, 'Introduction', *October* 124, (Summer 2008), pp. 3-7, esp. p. 3.

3   The concerns of Italian art during the 1960s and 70s make themselves felt in the works of Francesco Vezzoli, with the films of Pier Paolo Paolini and his *Trilogia della vita* inspiring Vezzoli's Trilogia della Morte. Vezzoli comments on his childhood, saying that his mother's passion "had always been Pistoletto, but my parents also liked Mario Merz". p. 10 Francesco Vezzoli interviewed by Germano Celant, in the exh. cat. Francesco Vezzoli, *Trilogia della Morte* (Fondazione Prada, Milan) 2004, p. 11.

4   Duchamp, interview with Calvin Tomkins, quoted in Calvin Tompkins, *Duchamp: A Biography* (London: Pimlico, 1996), p. 231.

5   Rrose Sélavy act variously as the cover girl for his perfume; the signatory of Duchamp's *Monte Carlo Bond* in 1924, thirty copies of which were priced at 500 F, and investors were promised a 20 per cent. return over three years. The bonds were devised to fund Duchamp's gambling, and were issued from a company of which he and Rrose Sélavy were on the board, the 'author' of the auction catalogue for *Tableaux, aquarelles et dessins par Francis Picabia appartenant à M. Marcel Duchamp*, Hôtel Drouot, Paris in 1926, which contained eighty works by Picabia. The catalogue is designed by Duchamp; the preface is written by Duchamp and signed 'Rrose Sélavy',

6   Conversation with the author, Rome, 4 March 2009.

7   Piero Manzoni, 'Alcune realizzazioni – Alcuni esperimenti – Alcuni progetti,' text written in 1962, published in the magazine *Evoluzione delle Lettere e delle Arti* 1 (January 1963), republished in Germano Celant, ed., *Piero Manzoni* (Naples: Museo d'Arte Contemporanea Donnaregina, 2007), pp. 336-7, esp. p. 337.

8   See also Christopher Duggan and Christopher Wagstaff, eds., *Italy in the Cold War: Politics, Culture and Society* 1948-58 (Oxford and Washington D.C.: Berg Publishers Limited, 1995).

9   See Romano F. Cattaneo, 'Un campione del nostro tempo,' *Il Borghese* 38, Milan, 21 September 1961, p. 100. See also Guido Almansi, 'Fino all'ultimo sberleffo,' *La Repubblica*, Rome, 8 February 1990.

10   Lucy Lippard, *Six Years: The Dematerialisation of the Art Object* (Los Angeles and London: University of California Press, Berkeley, 1972).

11   Gilman, op. cit., p. 3.7

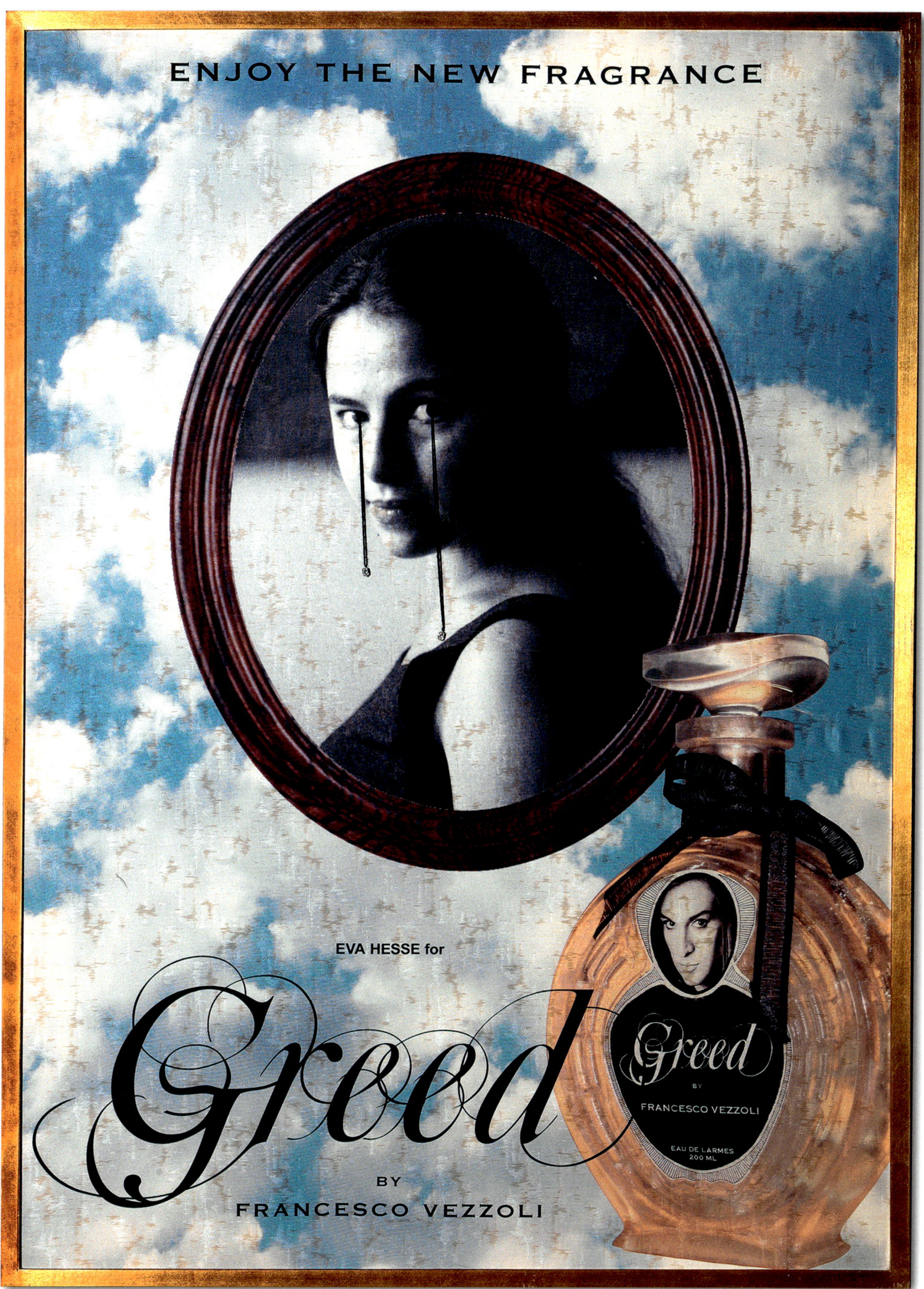

ENJOY THE NEW FRAGRANCE
EVA HESSE for
Greed
BY
FRANCESCO VEZZOLI
Greed
BY
FRANCESCO VEZZOLI
EAU DE LARMES
200 ML

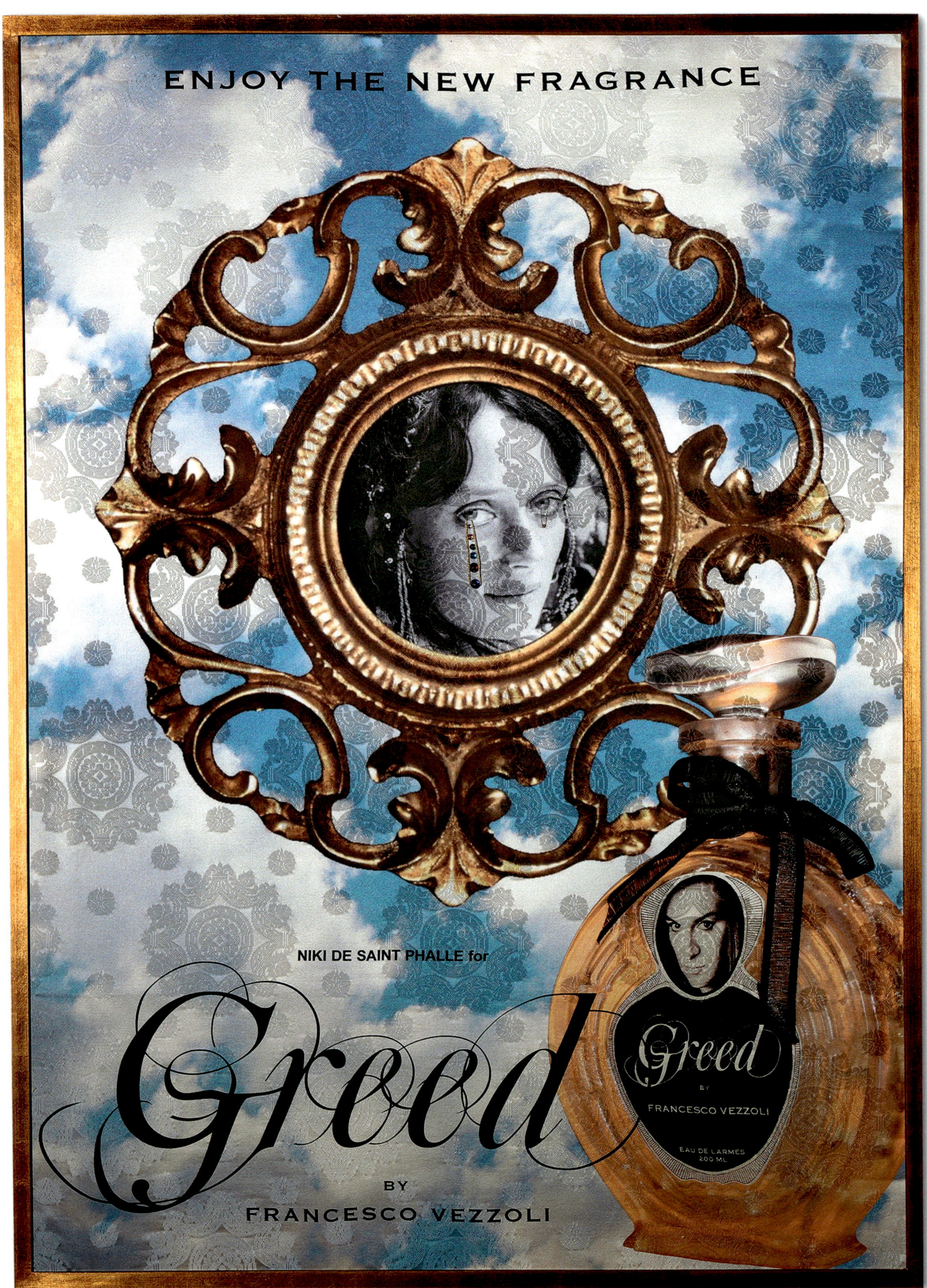

ENJOY THE NEW FRAGRANCE
NIKI DE SAINT PHALLE for
Greed
BY
FRANCESCO VEZZOLI
Greed
BY
FRANCESCO VEZZOLI
EAU DE LARMES
200 ML

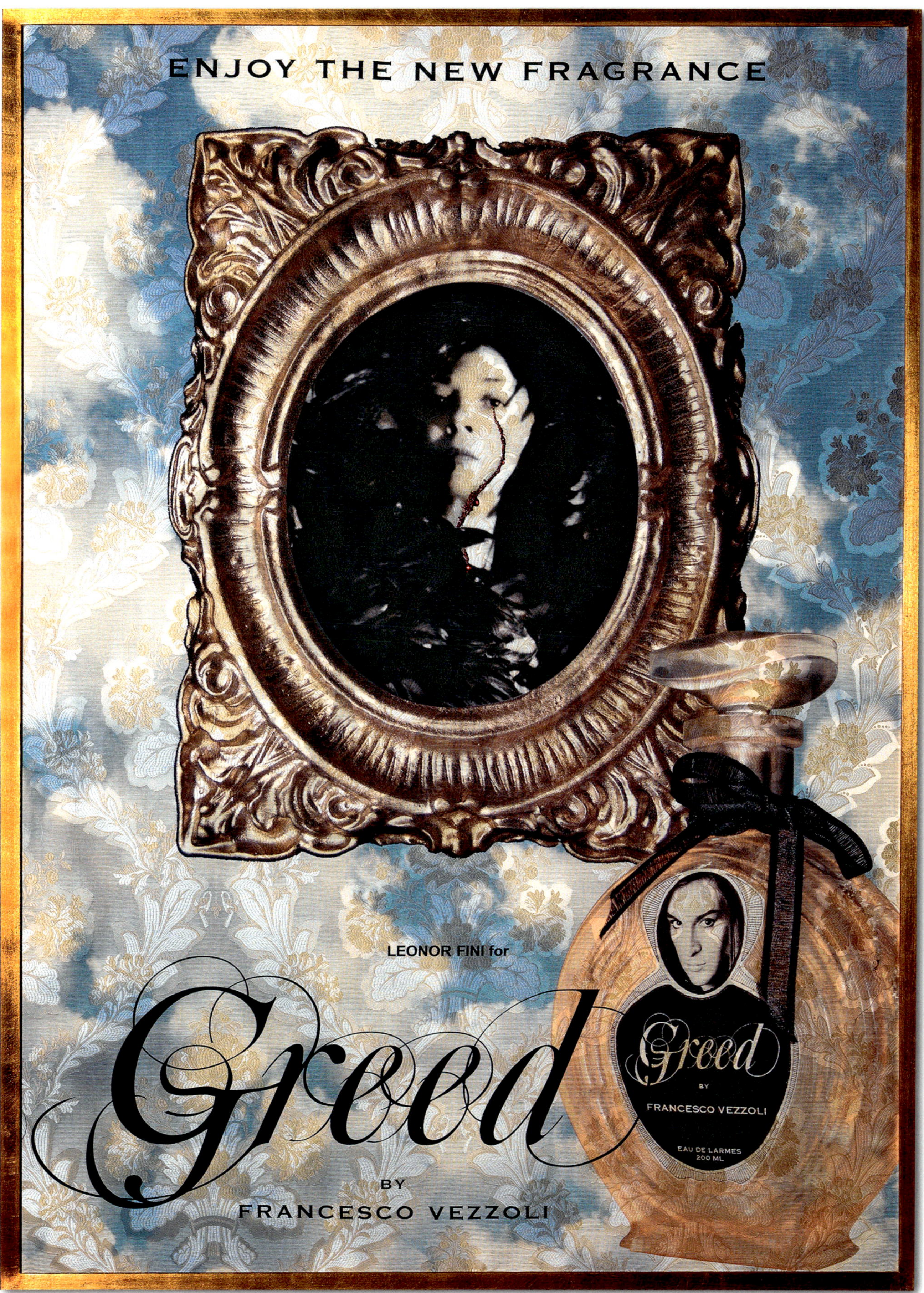

ENJOY THE NEW FRAGRANCE
LEONOR FINI for
Greed
BY
FRANCESCO VEZZOLI
Greed
BY
FRANCESCO VEZZOLI
EAU DE LARMES
200 ML

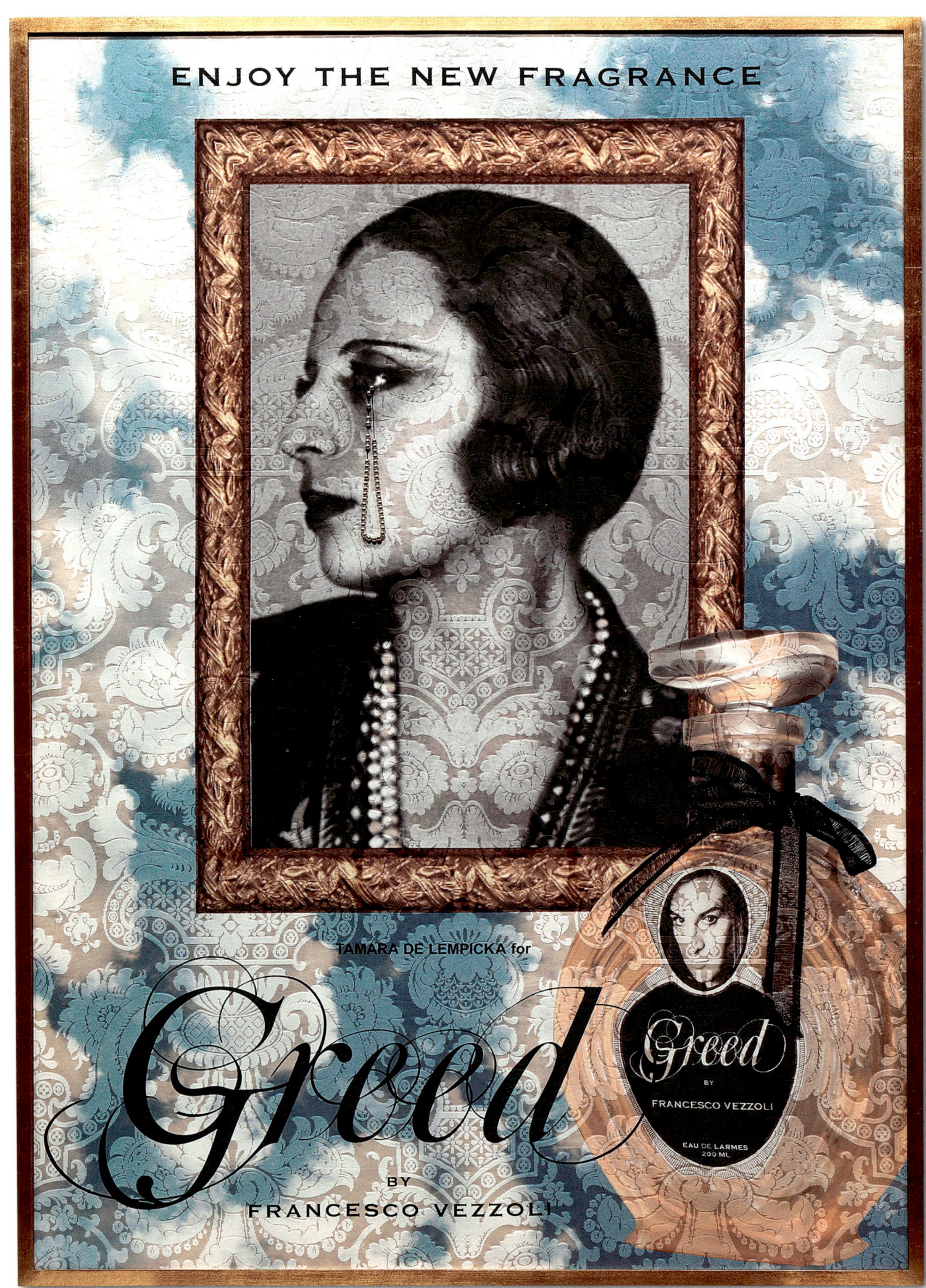

ENJOY THE NEW FRAGRANCE
TAMARA DE LEMPICKA for
Greed
BY
FRANCESCO VEZZOLI
Greed
BY
FRANCESCO VEZZOLI
EAU DE LARMES
200 ML

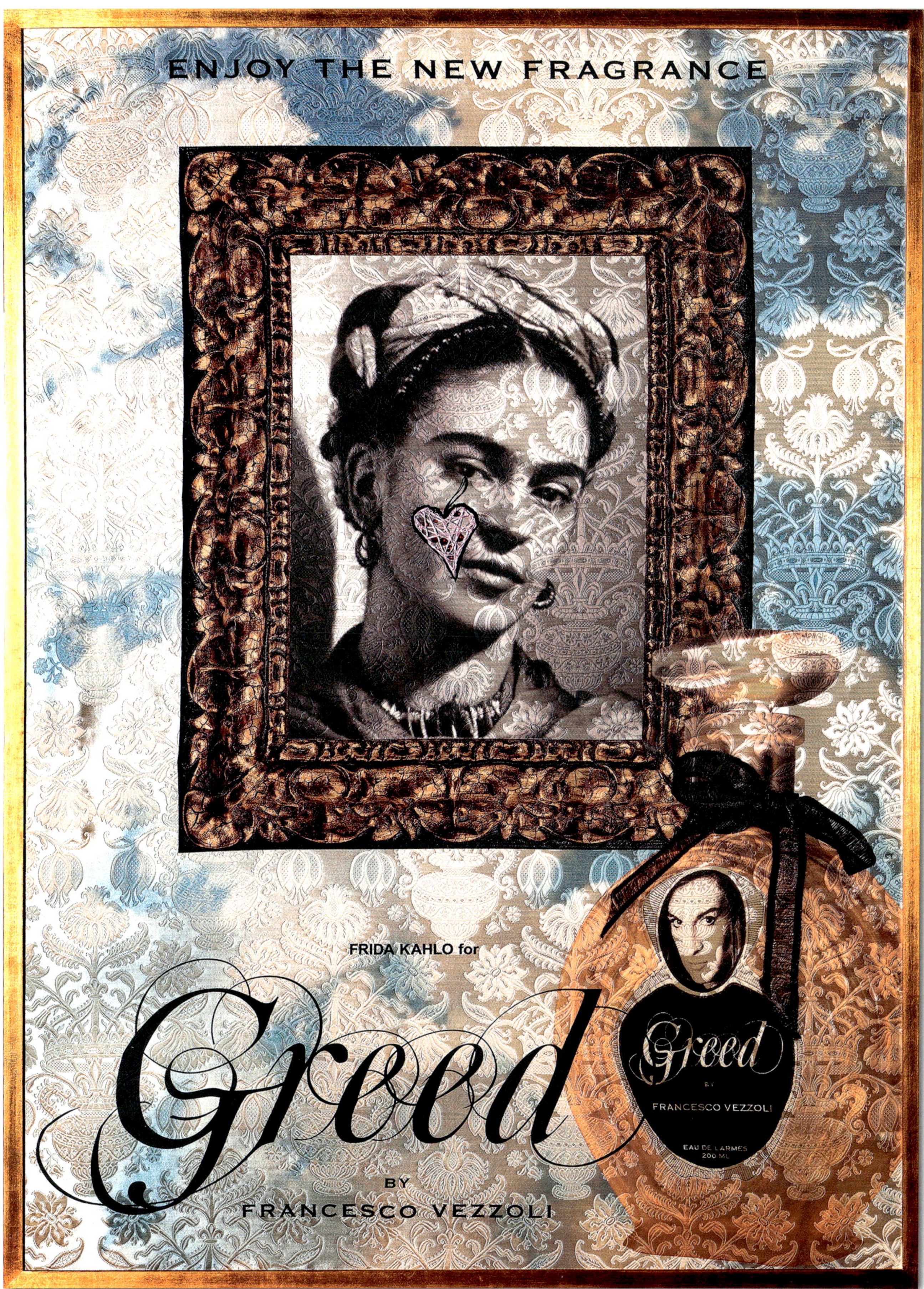

ENJOY THE NEW FRAGRANCE
FRIDA KAHLO for
Greed
BY
FRANCESCO VEZZOLI
Greed
BY
FRANCESCO VEZZOLI
EAU DE LARMES
200 ML

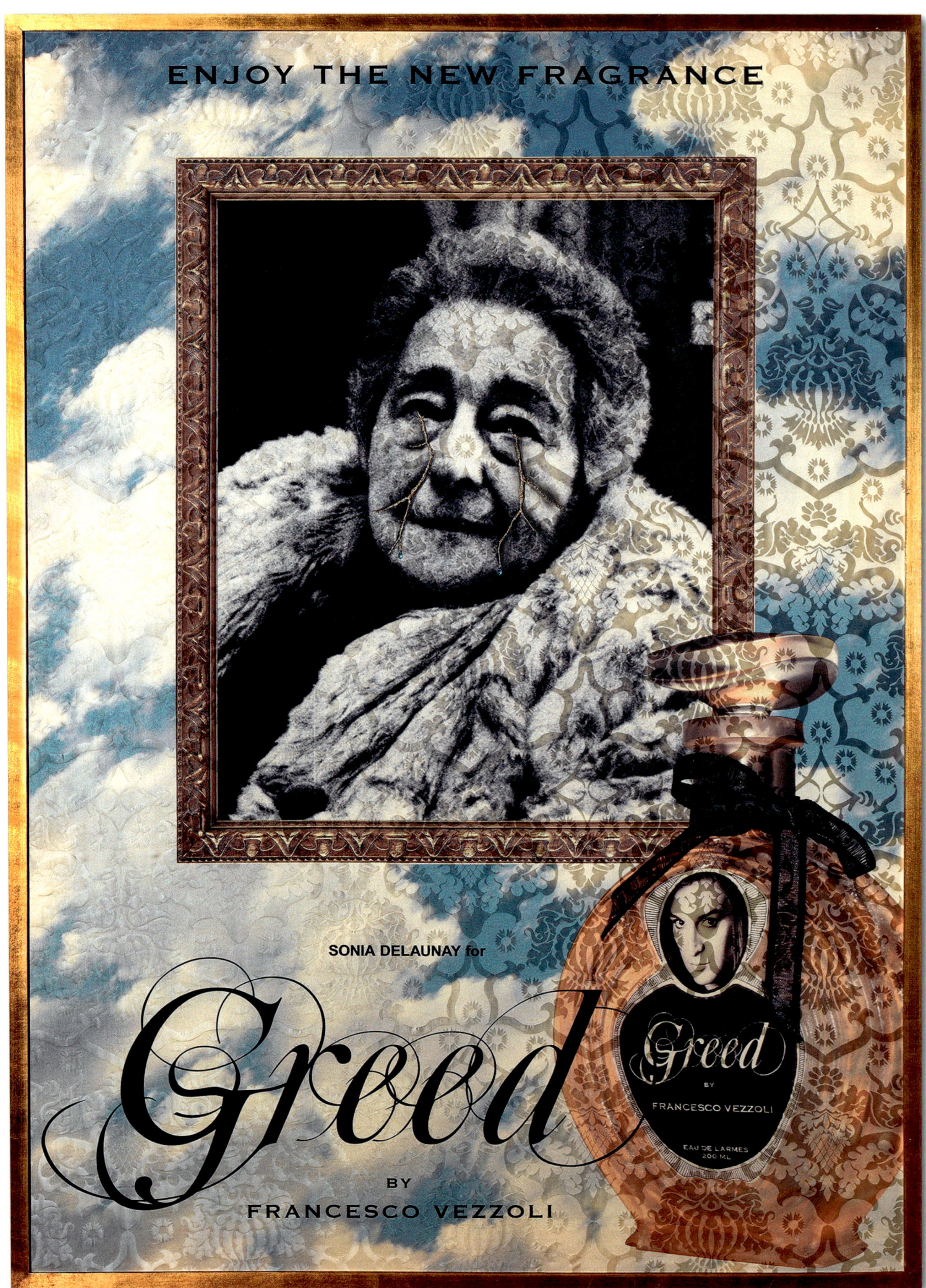

ENJOY THE NEW FRAGRANCE
SONIA DELAUNAY for
Greed
BY
FRANCESCO VEZZOLI
Greed
BY
FRANCESCO VEZZOLI
EAU DE LARMES
200 ML

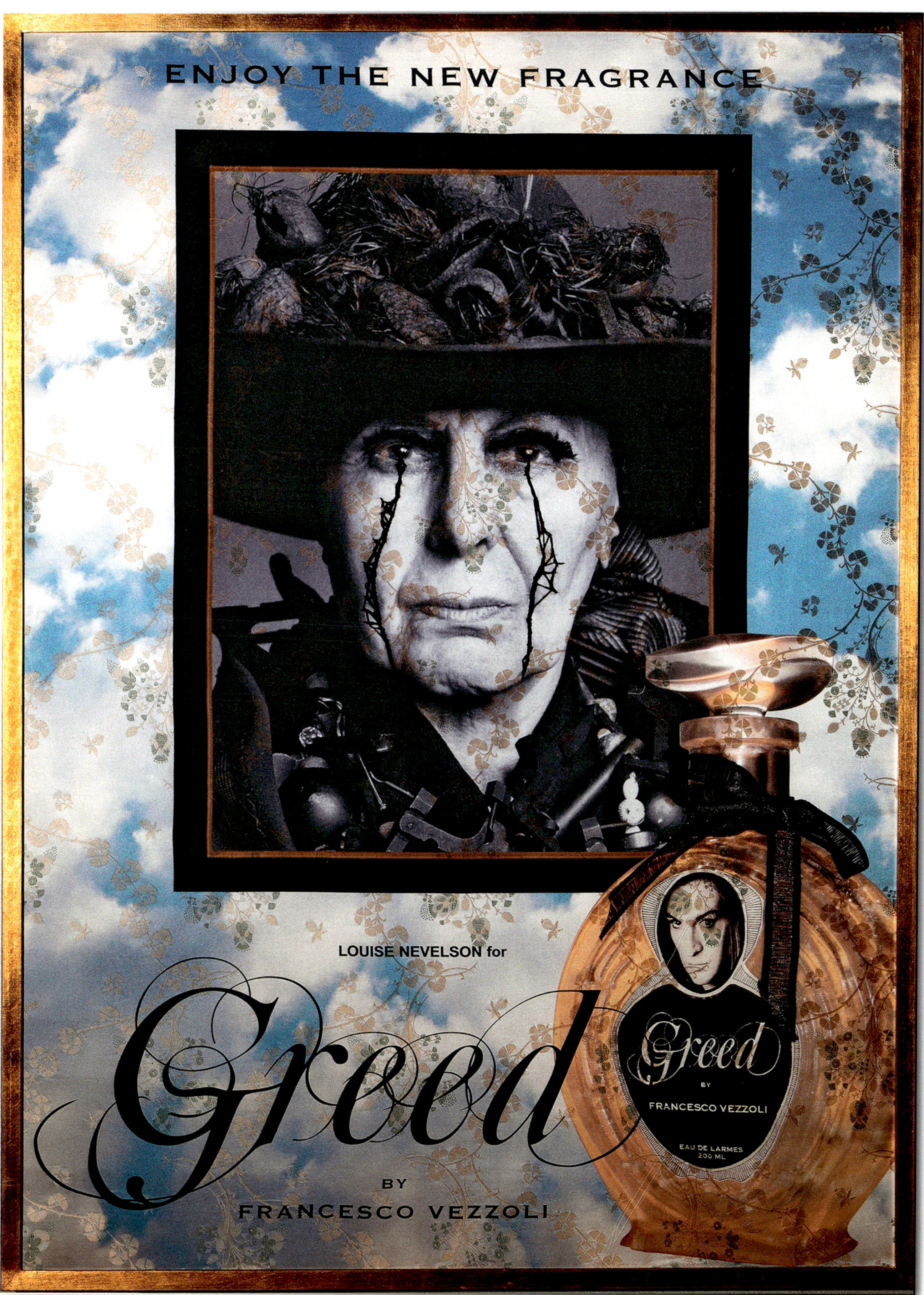

ENJOY THE NEW FRAGRANCE
LOUISE NEVELSON for
Greed
BY
FRANCESCO VEZZOLI
Greed
BY
FRANCESCO VEZZOLI
EAU DE LARMES
200 ML

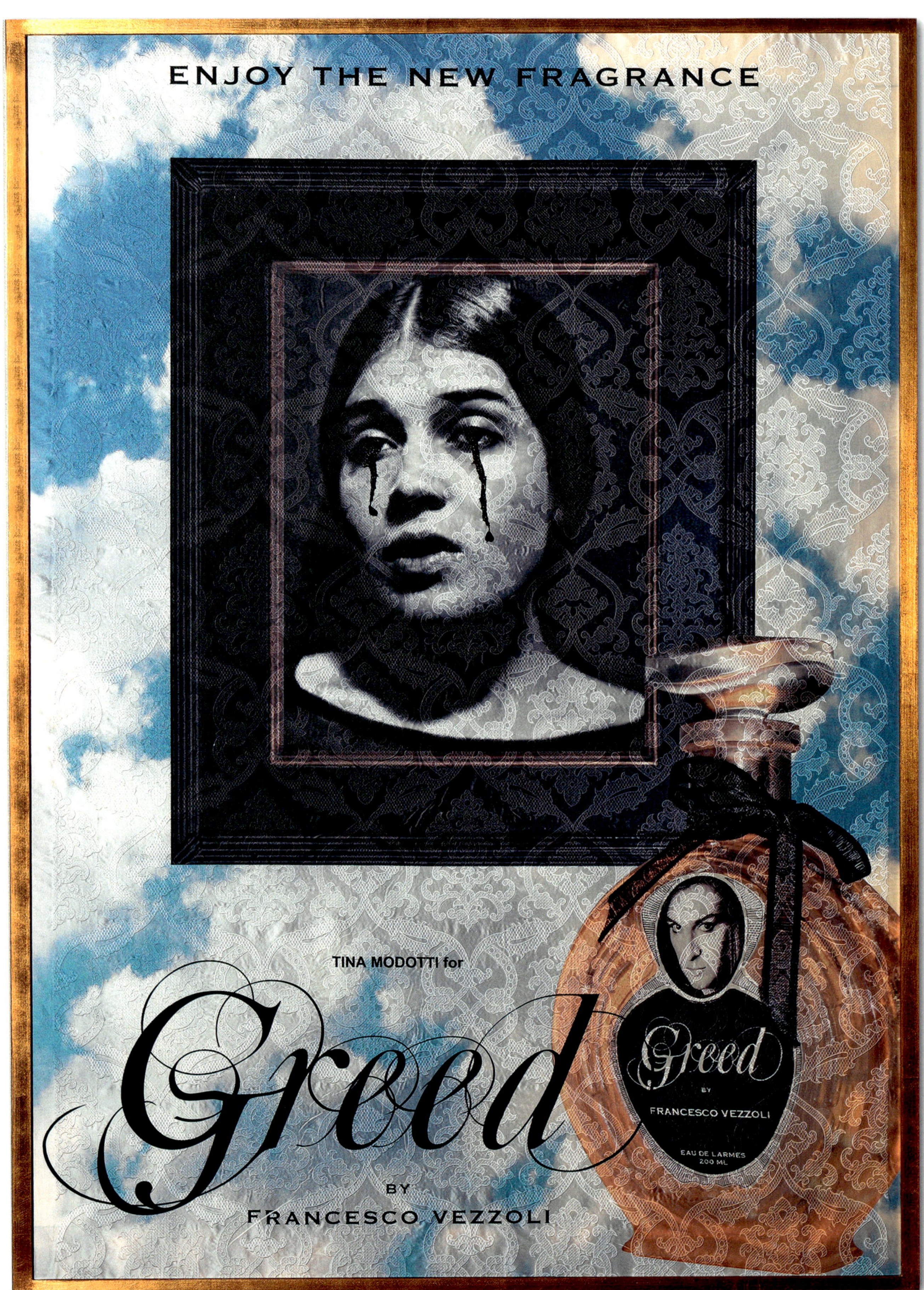

ENJOY THE NEW FRAGRANCE
TINA MODOTTI for
Greed
BY
Francesco Vezzoli
Greed
BY
FRANCESCO VEZZOLI
EAU DE LARMES
200 ML

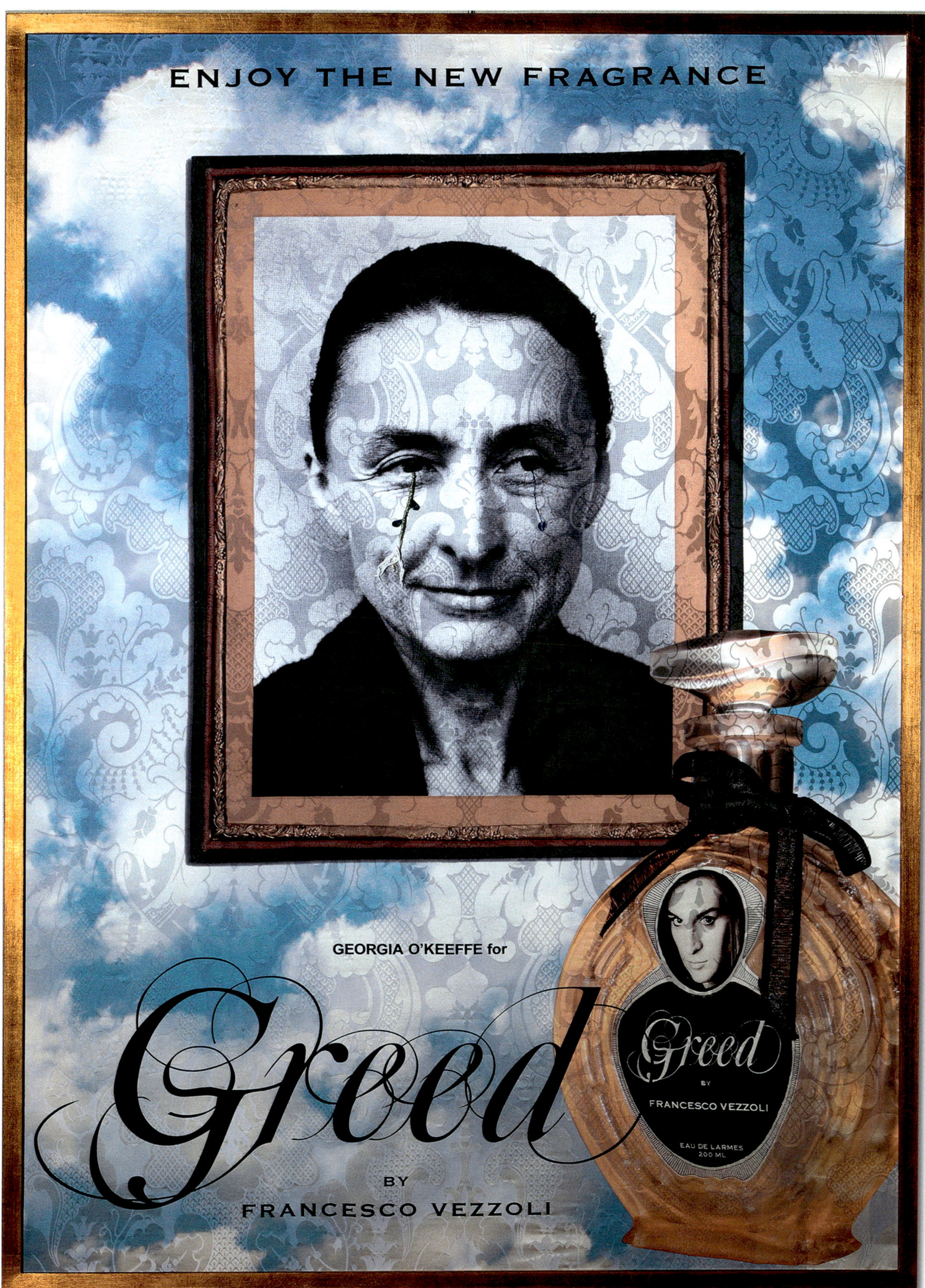

ENJOY THE NEW FRAGRANCE
GEORGIA O'KEEFFE for
Greed
BY
FRANCESCO VEZZOLI
Greed
BY
FRANCESCO VEZZOLI
EAU DE LARMES
200 ML

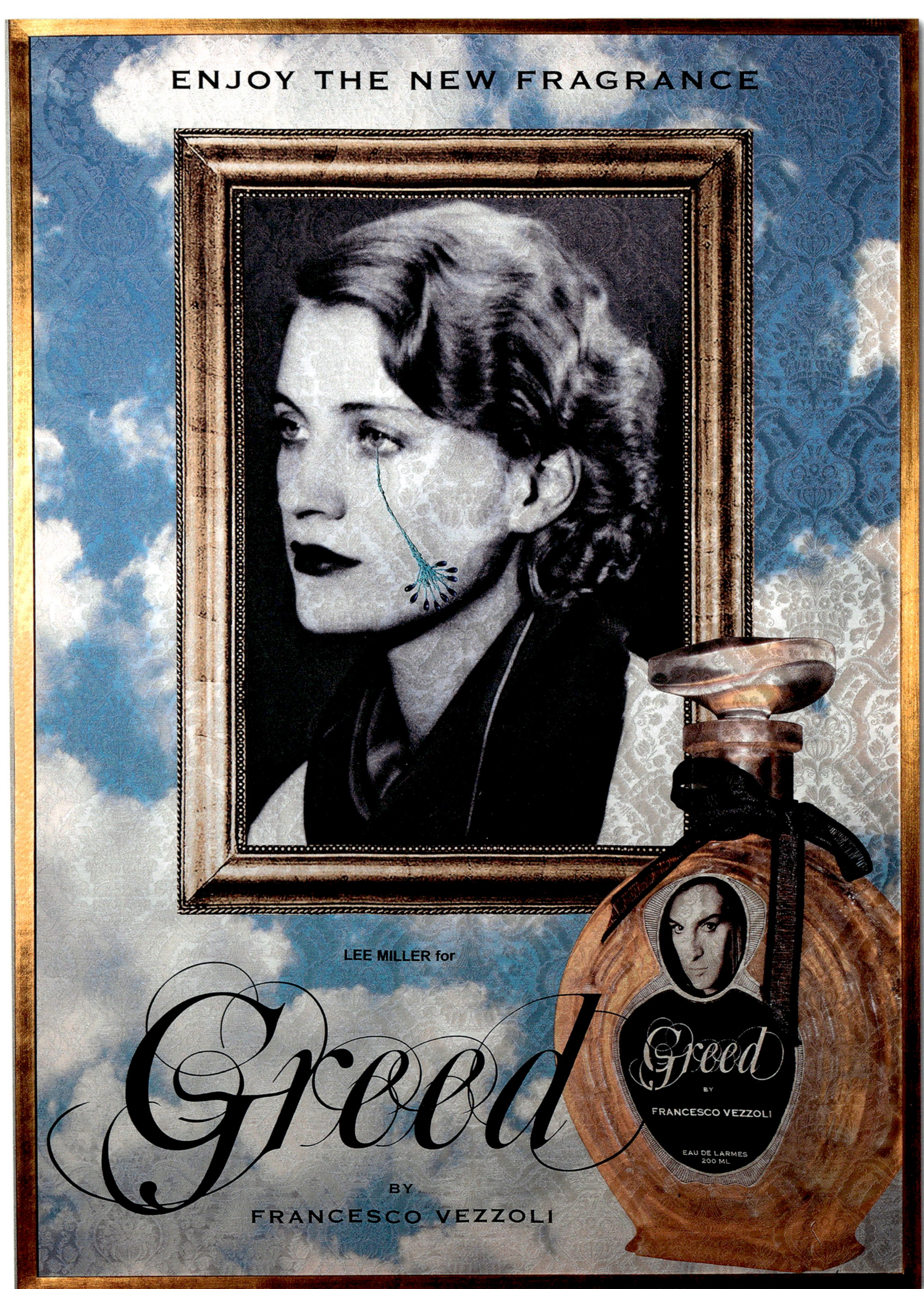

ENJOY THE NEW FRAGRANCE
LEE MILLER for
Greed
BY
FRANCESCO VEZZOLI
Greed
BY
FRANCESCO VEZZOLI
EAU DE LARMES
200 ML

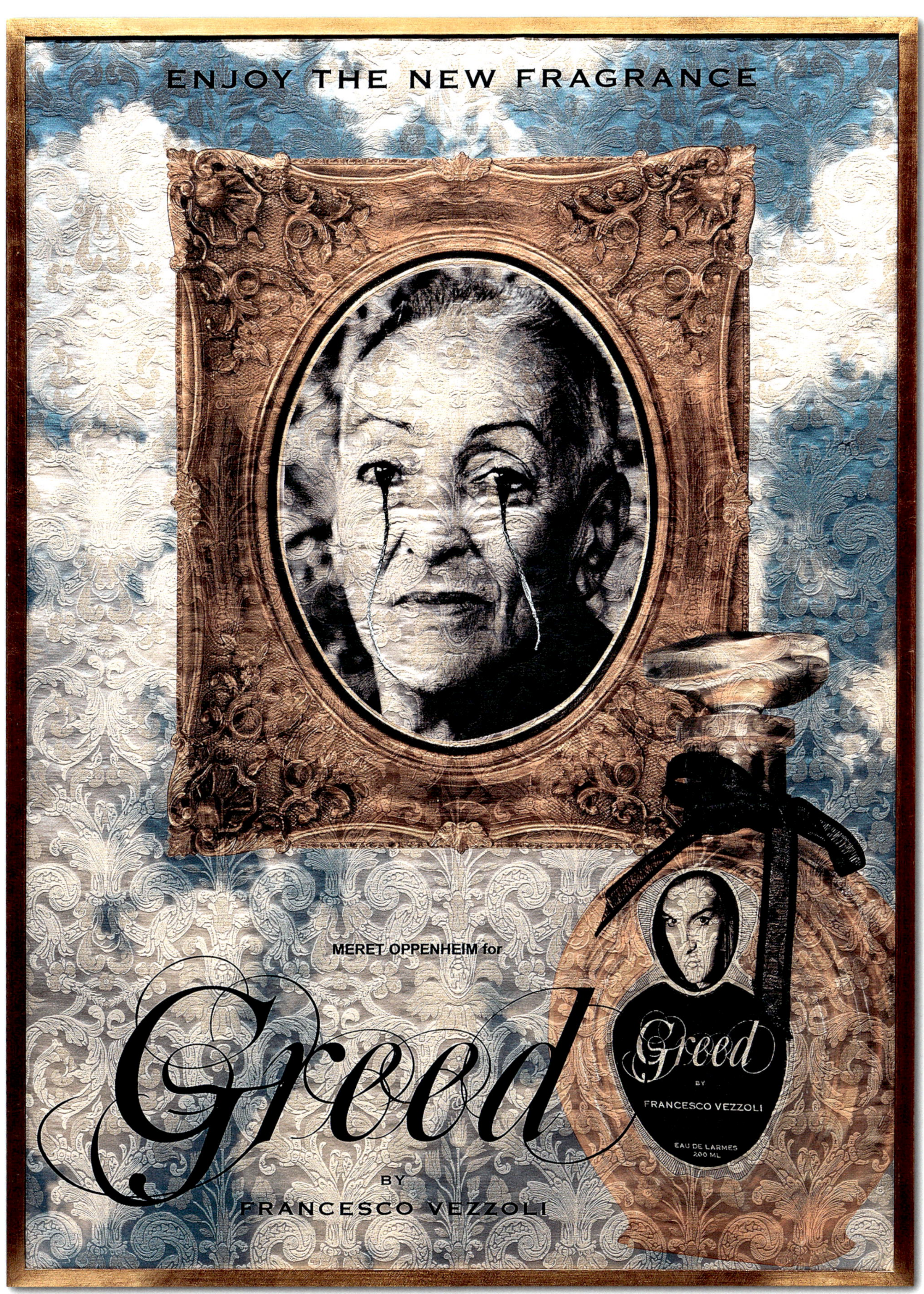

ENJOY THE NEW FRAGRANCE
MERET OPPENHEIM for
Greed
BY
FRANCESCO VEZZOLI
Greed
BY
FRANCESCO VEZZOLI
EAU DE LARMES
200 ML

Just after the shooting of *Greed*, in October 2009, Roman Polanski sat down with Francesco Vezzoli and Christoper Bollen from *Interview* in his Paris office—decorated with photographs and a broken Eames chair—to smoke a Cuban cigar and discuss his film heroes, his fight with Faye Dunaway, and why *Wanted and Desired* brings him some degree of closure.

CHRISTOPHER BOLLEN: What kind of cigars do you smoke?

ROMAN POLANSKI: The best. Mainly Montecristo. We only have Cuban cigars here, you see. Not like in America. [*pauses*] You know, I did an interview for *Interview* with Andy back in 1973.

CB: I think, in fact, you did two with him. Do you remember the questions he asked you?

RP: Not at all. He didn't care. In those times, Andy was doing it just to do it. He didn't care whether the interview was interesting or not.

FRANCESCO VEZZOLI: In your autobiography [*Roman by Polanski*] there is a passage about how Andy and his group descended on the villa you had in Rome in the early '70s. That's quite a group of houseguests.

RP: Yeah, but they were a very quiet group. They were not rambunctious or anything. And Andy had such gentle manners and was always saying he liked everything: "Oh, that's great," or "That's wonderful." He always had good things to say about everything and everybody. That was his personality.

FV: Or his strategy. Who was there with him? Was Paul Morrissey there?

RP: Yes. And Morrissey was just the opposite. He was very critical. I remember one thing he said that really surprised me at the time, but I have begun to think he is 100 percent right. He said that you should legalize all the hard drugs and just put them on the market. This is absolutely right. It's completely absurd when you think about it. It's a Third World business and just promotes crime. I don't think that there would be more users if drugs were legalized. I don't know anyone who is not using drugs for the reason that they're illegal.

CB: Right. And you could tax them.

RP: Tax them! Tax them and use the money for the education against them.

FV: That's a wonderful way to start the interview. I remember reading that once in London in the '60s you were depressed and you took LSD. Do you remember the experience?

RP: Yes. [*laughs*] I remember it very well.

FV: The first time you and I met was at a dinner party. You were telling me that London for you in the '60s wasn't just the happiest moment in *your* life, it was the happiest moment for the world.

RP: I think so. Definitely. It was a time of great aspirations and hopes and joy in general.

FV: You don't see any of that in the world now?

RP: I see the contrary, really.

FV: Obviously the scene around you in London at that time had a lot to do with your happiness. In the final lines of your autobiography you wrote, "What drove me to take my fantasy world and turn it into a real one? Was it the sexual urge that had somehow been at the root of it all? Was it that I would never have met all the women I dreamed of possessing had I remained an undersize inhabitant of the Krakow ghetto or a peasant boy from Wysoka?" I like that, even remotely, you think that your whole career could be explained by a sexual drive.

RP: There is a Russian proverb: "You will never fuck all women of the world, but you should try."

FV: Did you try?

RP: No, I didn't. But you have to take it into consideration, nevertheless.

FV: I'm sure you know the movie by [François] Truffaut called *The Man Who Loved Women* [1977]. There is a character who falls for every girl he meets. But the only one he really falls in love with is the one who doesn't return his love. Basically it refers to the obsession Truffaut had with

Catherine Deneuve. Truffaut was with you at Cannes during the May '68 uprisings.

RP: Truffaut called me one morning and said that I must come to a meeting to discuss what to do about Henri Langlois. Langlois was the head of the Cinémathèque. He was someone very popular and someone I personally liked very much. He had just been dismissed by Malraux, the Minister of Culture. Strangely enough, that started the whole thing. But even in that instance, when I arrived at the Palais des Festivals where this meeting was held in the festival's smaller screening room, I realized it had nothing to do with Langlois—it was simply a lot of left-wingers trying to dismantle the festival. It reminded me of certain moments of the Stalinist period in Poland, and Godard immediately attacked me. He was a fervent Trotskyist at that time, and, well, he was many things . . . That was probably the period when being a Trotskyist was fashionable. I saw a lot of people in this room who had nothing even to do with the festival. They didn't have films to present nor had they been invited. They said, "The festival is over. It's over. We don't want it. We don't want a festival of stars . . ."

FV: No more stars.

RP: They said, "We want a festival of dialogue." I said, "So create some kind of colloquium." I remember Louis Malle was among those voices wanting to do away with the festival—the next year he had a film in competition there! And two years later again! So you see the hypocrisy of those people.

FV: Of all the nouvelle vague directors, whose work were you closest to?

RP: Truffaut. Definitely.

FV: Is it because at a certain stage of his career, he admitted a more relaxed and open relationship with American cinema and his passion for Hitchcock?

RP: It's not because of that. It's that his passion for Hitchcock and his interest in American cinema must have something to do with his idea of the movies. I think that he had a different basis and a real talent. I liked him as a person and I liked him as an artist. At that period, he was the only French member of the so-called nouvelle vague that I would appreciate. Some of the films of the nouvelle vague were excruciatingly boring. Most of them were completely amateurish. It was just one of those periods when suddenly people get ecstatic about something which may later prove to be completely worthless or fake. It was a little bit of the emperor's new clothes.

FV: You were close to Otto Preminger, too, right?

RP: Yeah. I liked Otto very much.

FV: And he was not loved by the people of the nouvelle vague.

RP: He was not loved by many people, including those who worked for him. He was apparently tyrannical. But he was loved by his friends. I remember Mike Nichols was always very keen on him. These times, both in London and in Hollywood, were periods when you would see a lot of each other— unlike now. I hardly meet anyone working in film anymore. In those times, parties and restaurants and clubs would be places where people would gather, and you could really meet and entertain some kinds of relationships.

FV: Do you think that doesn't happen now because it is all a corporate event?

RP: It's simply a different climate. I sometimes feel that I don't live in the same world.

FV: But somehow you've been capable of remaining the epitome of cool for 40 years.

RP: I don't know about that. Maybe.

FV: I decide that. Let me do something for today.

CB: Do you think having that kind of close relationship with other actors and directors and producers was helpful for making your own films?

RP: It was helpful to maintain a certain kind of atmosphere, a mood which is creative in general. It's inspiring. It's positive.

FV: You're right. That doesn't happen anymore.

RP: No, it doesn't. In certain circles it still happens—I think more in fashion than in anything else.

CB: Even from a distance, do you sense that those relationships have changed in Hollywood as well?

RP: That's what I've been told. It's difficult for me to have a valid opinion. But from many friends who I see all the time, who either work or spend time in Hollywood, they say that it's an entirely different era. Mainly the business has changed. It's no longer run by capable individuals, but by some kind of committee. There are no more one-person decisions. It's decision by committee. It's flat in general.

FV: Who is the Robert Evans of today?

RP: Who is it? I don't know. They recruit from an entirely different background. They're mainly the golden boys or the baby boomers who moved into this industry, and they're looking for something entirely different. They are really interested in numbers and figures. They want to protect themselves.

FV: Even intellectually, they don't want to be confronted by anything.

RP: I don't think they even consider intellectualism.

CB: Do you think the movies you make would be entirely different if you shot them in Hollywood?

RP: Well, this is all supposition. Certainly different, because you are what you eat, as they say. But I think I would have been able to resist some of the traps my colleagues have fallen into.

FV: Something that happened three days ago came to my mind. Ennio De Concini, the screenwriter, just died. I know you often quote from the Italian cinema of the '50s and '60s.

RP: There were so many Italian directors whose films we were always impatiently awaiting—De Sica, Visconti, Fellini, Cavalcanti, Mario Monicelli. They were fabulous movies, and there were great Italian screenwriters, like Zavattini and Suso Cecchi d'Amico.

FV: I filmed my second video in Suso Cecchi d'Amico's house. She has this big couch that is all embroidered by Silvana Mangano. You remember Silvana?

RP: Of course. I knew Silvana. She was with Dino De Laurentiis, and Dino is a friend of mine. Dino wanted me to do a film for him called *Hurricane*. It never happened, although we took several trips to Bora Bora, and Silvana

came along. I spent a lot of time with them, or with her, traveling. But I first
met her long before that. I went to a festival in Cartagena [Spain], and she
was invited there. I remember her very much for one thing: It was cloudy,
and some black guy on the beach sold me a little bottle of coconut oil,
telling me that I'll get a suntan in spite of these clouds. So I put this stuff all
over myself. Not only did I get the suntan, but I burned myself to the extent
that I couldn't even put a T-shirt on. Silvana said that a frequent application
of alcohol helps. And I can tell you this is true. If it ever happens to you, put
alcohol on the sunburned skin, and it goes away. You have to keep putting it
on every half hour.

FV: She certainly never got sunburned.

RP: She stayed away from the sun. She told me I was stupid. And she was
right.

FV: Did you find her beautiful?

RP: She was extremely beautiful.

FV: I'm sorry. I'm obsessed with her. She was the coolest actress the Italian
cinema has ever had.

RP: Yes. And elegant.

FV: You know this anecdote that when she would go to Capucci to have her
dresses made, she would commission three of the same one, and during
dinners she would go upstairs, pretending she was just going to powder her
nose, then come back down wearing what looked like the same dress but
it was a new one, just so she would stay immaculate. [*Polanski laughs*] I've
always been fascinated by somebody who was seductive but not in a sexual
way.

RP: You say she wasn't sexy? I don't think I've seen a sexier actress than
Silvana in *Riso Amaro* [1949].

FV: I watched *Chinatown* last night. It reminded me that you are possibly
the only heir to Orson Welles.

RP: That's very flattering, because he was my complete idol for years, and
still is.

FV: When I watch *Chinatown*, I feel *Touch of Evil* [1958]. For me it has this kind of hopelessness about evil that you see in *Touch of Evil*. Maybe it's the period, maybe it's the open cars.

RP: It's really accidental, because I did not at all have any kind of reference to it. In *Chinatown* what I was trying to create was this Philip Marlowe atmosphere, which I'd never seen in the movies the way I got it in the books of Dashiell Hammett or Raymond Chandler. As a young man, I loved that literature of that particular period. That's what I wanted to re-create. But I didn't think of any film that I could refer to.

FV: I'm saying that I think you achieved the same level of darkness. I meant that as a compliment.
Every time I see *Chinatown*, when it gets toward the end, I cry. I really do. I start crying.

RP: Really? Well, it should be moving. If I can evoke such a reaction in the spectator, I am very happy. But I sometimes cry in the moments that are not necessarily dramatic or tragic in the films, often because of the music. I wonder whether it's the music that has that effect on you in this film.

CB: You had to re-score *Chinatown*, didn't you?

RP: Yeah.

FV: And you had to change the director of photography, as well.

RP: Yeah, at the beginning I had the guy who did *The Magnificent Ambersons* [1942]. But he wasn't up to it anymore and didn't evolve with the rest of cinema. It was a difficult moment. Bob Evans wanted me to make the change, and he was right.

FV: But he also wanted Jane Fonda to play the lead.

CB: It's very hard to imagine Jane Fonda doing Faye Dunaway's role. It would have been more *Klute* [1971] than Marlowe.

RP: Here I dug my heels in.

CB: You're glad you picked Faye Dunaway, even though she was so notoriously difficult on set?

RP: Well, I mean, who cares? To the audience it doesn't really matter how much the director struggled with an actor. It's the result that counts. In this book by David O. Selznick [*Memo from David O. Selznick*, 2000], he wrote that "the only thing that counts is the final result."

CB: It doesn't matter how hard it was to get there.

RP: That's right.

FV: It doesn't matter how many hairs you had to pull out of her head.

RP: [*laughs*] It doesn't matter what the reaction was.

CB: I love that after you plucked one of Faye's hairs out because it was catching light, her response was to scream, "I don't believe it. That motherfucker pulled my hair out!" And she stormed off set. [*Polanski laughs*] Did you ever talk to Faye Dunaway after *Chinatown*?

RP: Oh, yeah. Of course. Last time I saw her was in Cannes last year. She was also giving a prize. We met in the bathroom. I was washing my hands, and some woman was washing her hands, and she said, "Hi, Roman." I look up in the mirror, and it was Faye.

CB: You say all the trouble is worth the result. I have to tell you that there is a single shot in *Rosemary's Baby* that has always blown me away. It's during the scene when Mia Farrow is passing out just before she's raped by the devil. She's drugged out and closes her eyes, and you see her floating on a raft in this beautiful blue sea. It only plays for a second, but it always struck me: How did Polanski get Mia Farrow on a raft in a blue sea and only show a second of that footage? That's a lot of effort for something so quick.

RP: It was always for a second. It doesn't matter how long. If it stays with you, that's what matters. If you make it last any longer, you start analyzing the elements and also the way it was put together, and the charm is gone.

CB: I've seen *Rosemary's Baby* probably 60 times.

RP: Really?

CB: Yeah. *Rosemary's Baby* is one of the things I'll remember when I leave the world. Do you have any movies that you've watched a zillion times over?

RP: No, not compulsively. Because when I really love a movie, I don't want to spoil it by too frequent visits. But I like to come back to certain films, which I admire, like *Hamlet* [1948] with Laurence Olivier, like *Odd Man Out* [1947] by Carol Reed, like *Citizen Kane* [1941]. *Citizen Kane*—that film does not age at all. You know what I like to see again and again? *Snow White* [1937].

CB: The Disney cartoon?

RP: Oh, it's beautiful! I don't think they make anything better. The charm of this film is just unbelievable, and this naïveté. It's so naïvely beautiful. What is it, corny or something? But I just love this movie. When have you seen it last?

CB: I haven't seen it since I was a kid.

FV: Me neither.

RP: Watch it. Watch it together.

CB: You could remake it . . .

RP: I couldn't do it any better. What's the point?

FV: I like your anecdotes about when they asked you to do the remake of *Knife in the Water* [1962]. That was the year that you were competing with Fellini for the Oscar [Best Foreign Language Film].

RP: That's right. It was right after that that those two guys from 20th Century Fox, John Shepridge and . . . what was the other one's name . . . I don't remember his name, it will come back later . . . They called me to the office. I thought they were going to offer me some fantastic job, which I needed desperately. They told me that they would like me to redo *Knife in the Water*. I mean, it would be an exercise in self-sodomy, you know?

CB: You've given so many actresses their defining roles. Mia Farrow did a lot of Woody Allen movies that were great, but *Rosemary's Baby* I still think is her defining role.

RP: It was her first motion picture. Before that, she only did television.

CB: *Peyton Place* . . . Did you originally want her for *Rosemary's Baby*?

RP: Well, it was more Robert Evans's idea, because I really didn't know her that well. But he was convinced that she would be great, and I went along with it. I met her, and I thought, Okay, fine.

CB: I read somewhere that you wanted to use that actress . . . oh, what's her name . . . she later starred in *Play It As It Lays* [1972].

RP: Tuesday Weld. I wanted a sort of healthier-looking young woman, like a typical milk-fed American that a couple like the Castevets would be really convinced was good material for a mother—which Mia was not necessarily. But it was a good choice. And it was a terrific time, those few months of work with Mia. She was fantastic to work with.

CB: What's weird is, she's become the ultimate mother since then.

RP: I don't know how many she's got. Fourteen?

FV: Was it Vidal Sassoon who cut her hair short?

RP: Well, I knew Vidal. He was part of that London crowd in those times. We brought him to Los Angeles to cut her hair and made a big deal out of it—you know, invited the press, and so many press accepted the invitation that they had to put bleachers around when he was giving her the haircut. During all that time her hair was being clipped, she was talking about the Indians and other problems that were fashionable at that time.

CB: Are there any actors you worked with in the past who you'd like to work with again?

RP: Many. Unfortunately, my beloved actor, Jack MacGowran, died of flu in New York quite early in his life. He was in *Cul-de-Sac* [1966] and *The Fearless Vampire Killers* [1966].

FV: You should do another movie with Jack Nicholson.

RP: Jack, I enjoyed very much.

FV: You were the only one who could put him to good use. I feel so bad when they make him play the old man who goes after young girls . . .

CB: *The Bucket List* [2007] was shown on my flight to Paris. I didn't watch it.

RP: I haven't seen *The Bucket List*. For some reason, I don't know, I didn't feel at all like seeing that film.

CB: So many of your films are, in part, about the cities they are set in. *Repulsion* is very much about London. *Rosemary's Baby* is about New York. *Chinatown* is Los Angeles. *Frantic* is Paris. How important is the character of a city to your work?

RP: It's very important. It's very important to set your place in a concrete environment. I think Chekhov said that the important thing when you have a play or any kind of novel is to set the roots in a concrete place.

CB: How was it to work on Francesco's fragrance commercial? Was it good to work with Natalie Portman and Michelle Williams?

RP: It was tremendously inspiring. Both girls—Natalie and Michelle—were so charming and so easy, you know. It went so smoothly and all in one day that it was a real pleasure. They are very good actresses. Even in that little minute, in those few seconds, they were terrific.

CB: Lots of great directors do commercials. Like David Lynch did that Gucci fragrance commercial last year. Have you directed other commercials?

RP: Yeah, I have.

CB: Do you enjoy doing them?

RP: Sometimes. But not really. Usually you have this client and the agency and they talk about this product as if it was a marvel of the world . . .

FV: Like my perfume.

RP: But they take it seriously! Which is absolutely . . .

FV: Appalling.

RP: Appalling, yeah.

CB: You once said that if you could do it over again, you would do acting. Do you still think that?

RP: Yeah, I enjoyed acting very much. In fact, that's how I began. Those were my first steps—onstage, not in the movies. I am disappointed not doing more acting. But you have to learn lines, and it becomes more and more difficult . . . Do you know what I don't like about it? All this hurry-and-wait business. That's what it's all about. I admire actors for their infinite patience. That's why they need all those trailers and all their crowd of people who pamper them. But it is a drag to get up sometimes at 4:30 in the morning and get into makeup, and wait forever until they call you onto the set. On my side, it's different. It's excitement all the time, and I don't give a flying fuck whether they suffer or not, because at that moment I have to forget about their feelings and problems. Once on the set, I share their anxieties and I try to somehow deal with it. But for logistics, I have to overlook them . . .

CB: It's hard to overlook you as a personality as well. You're a director, but you have other interests, and your personal life has always been a big part of the Polanski legend.

RP: I simply think there's life after movies. I have to adhere to this philosophy, and therefore I like other things, and I have other passions. None are as big as movie-making, but they exist.

FV: Did you watch the documentary that Marina Zenovich did on you recently for HBO called *Roman Polanski: Wanted and Desired*?

RP: Yeah, yeah, I saw it.

FV: Is it okay if I ask you what was your opinion about it?

RP: Sure. Absolutely. I saw it and, first of all, I thought for the first time someone has told what happened. Everything else that has been written or shown about my problems were just myths that would be rehashed. The media uses the computer. They just get on there . . . When they have to write or something, they just get it on their screens, add a few sentences, and it becomes a snowball gathering around the same myth. And here she [Zenovich] took the pains of getting into the nitty-gritty of it, and got the material in the archives that I did not know even existed, and talked to the people who have never spoken about it. What comes out, among other things, in the documentary is the fact that one of the deputy district attorneys illegally influenced the judge—which, if it had been known at that time, would have caused the whole case to be thrown out in a week.

CB: When you heard about the film's being made, did you think, Oh, God, can we please get over the murders, the trial . . .

RP: Well, first I think she wrote me a letter, and I answered it, "I don't wish you to do the film." And I think she never got that or something. Then later she wanted to interview me. I never had any contact with her until the film was finished. Then she was in Paris, and my secretary asked me that now that the film is completed would I meet her? I said, "Of course. Now I can meet her." She asked me whether now I would let myself be interviewed, and I said that I wouldn't, because if the film is bad, what's the point of me contributing, and if it's good, there's even more reason for me not to be part of it, because everybody would think that it's some form of self-promotion. She agreed with me.

FV: I think that's the reason why the film is so powerful. Your absence makes the product politically powerful. You're exactly right. When you see it, you look like the biggest hero. And your absence makes it look even more so, because there are all these people who were really there explaining.

RP: Well, the district attorney says that he understands why I left. How you can say more?

CB: Do you feel very sour toward the media?

RP: Well, I always did, even before that, from the tragedy, you know, with Sharon [Tate, Polanski's wife, who was murdered by the Manson family in 1969]. That's the way I felt with the media. The way it was reported, the way it was commented on. That was quite a long time before my problems.

CB: Was Sharon's death the beginning of the media's becoming vultures around you? Did you expect a different reaction from the community?

RP: Before then I was sort of the toast of the town, you know, and then suddenly the media started amalgamating the murder with *Rosemary's Baby*, with my film . . . I mean, the simple-mindedness of those people is astonishing, even with all perspective of the time.

FV: There is this incapability of cutting a boundary between your movies and your private persona. It's incredible.

RP: It's incredible.

CB: Do you feel like the media here in Paris is much more respectful? Are they nicer to you?

RP: *Nice* is not the word. It's *correct*. And they leave me completely alone. They talk about my work and my films, and it's fine, you know?

FV: Do you like being alone?

RP: Well, I have moments. I like skiing, among other things, because I have moments when I am alone in the mountains. That's fantastic, when there's nobody around you. You see miles around you, and the sun is almost down . . .

FV: Have you ever skied at night?

RP: I have, yeah.

FV: It's beautiful.

RP: Yeah. Drunk also. Except that once I skied with a bunch of people, and everybody was drunk, and we had people carrying torches. There was a guy with an accordion, and I bumped into him, and they all started shouting at me, so I said, "Screw you," and I went off on my own. But then the torches ran off, and I found myself in a forest, at night, without any light, on skis, and that was not fun—particularly because I was drunk, as I said. Luckily at some point I started to see the light of the ski lift. I tell you, to be in the forest in the middle of the night, it's terrible.

FV: It's like a Polanski movie.

Originally published in *Interview*, February 2009, pp 98-105.

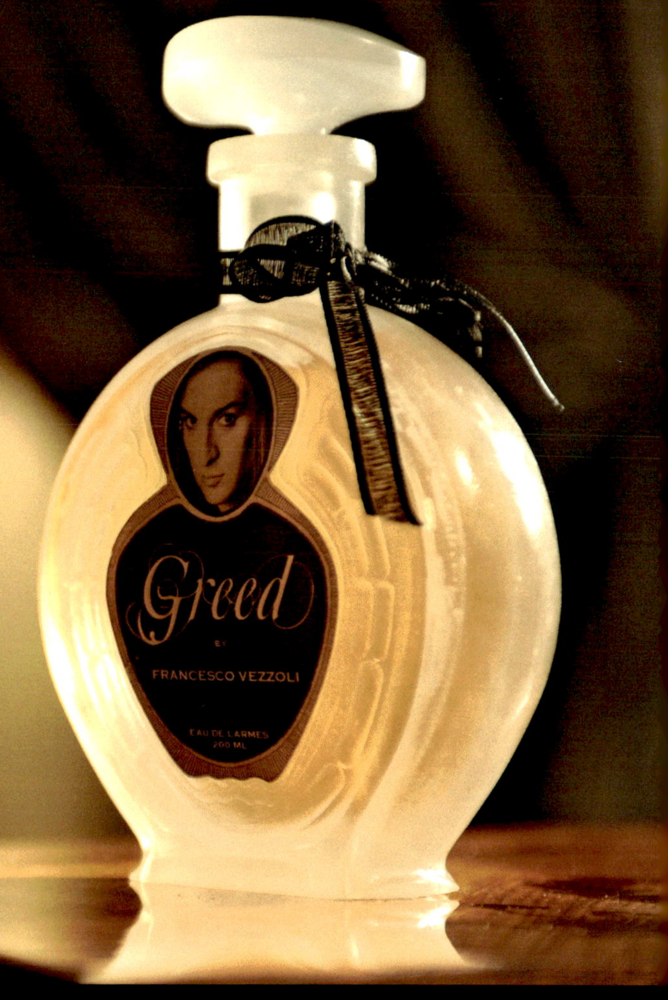

FRANCESCO
VEZZOLI

Greed

THE NEW FRAGRANCE

COMING SOON

Greed
BY
FRANCESCO VEZZOLI
EAU DE LARMES
200 ML

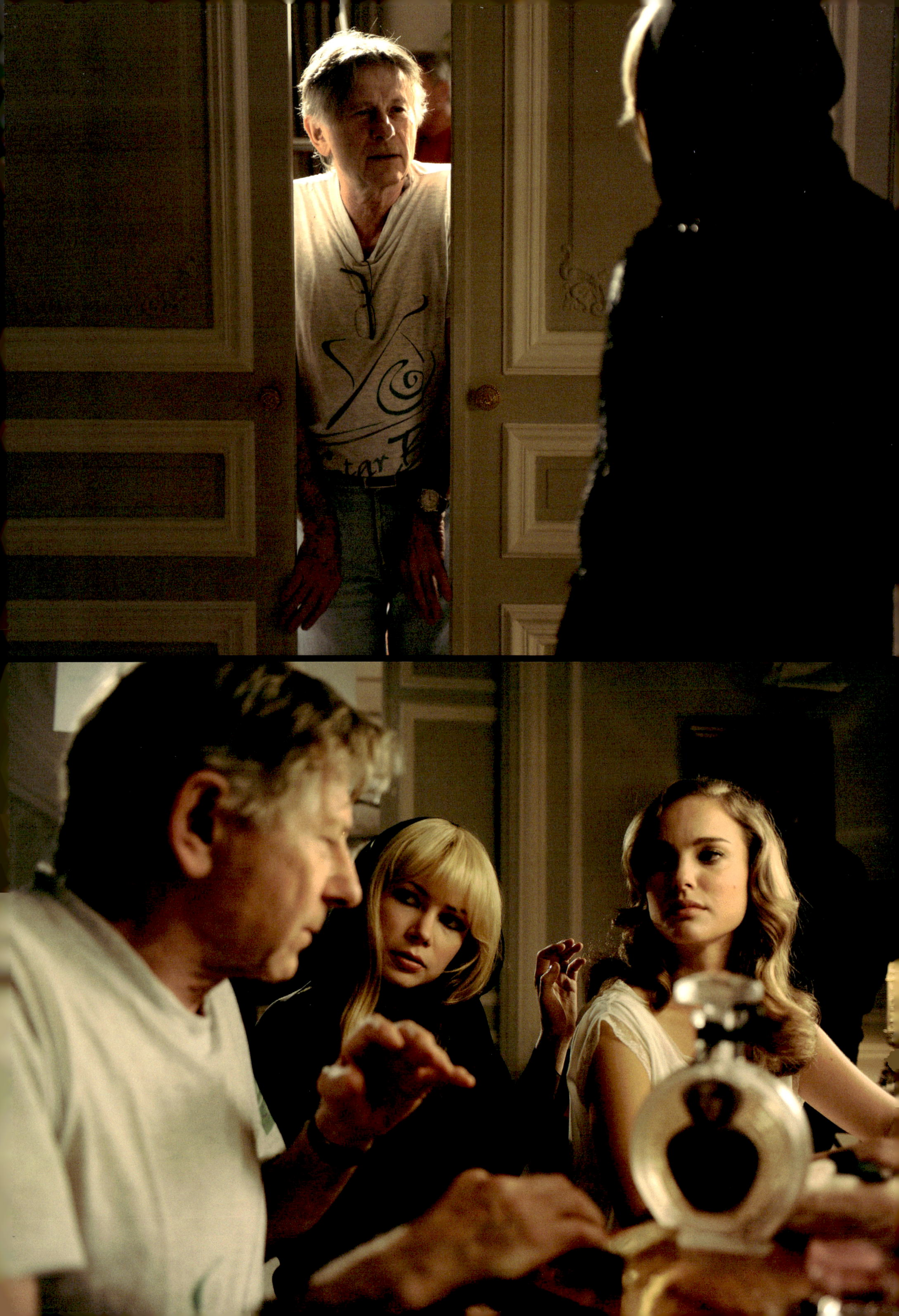

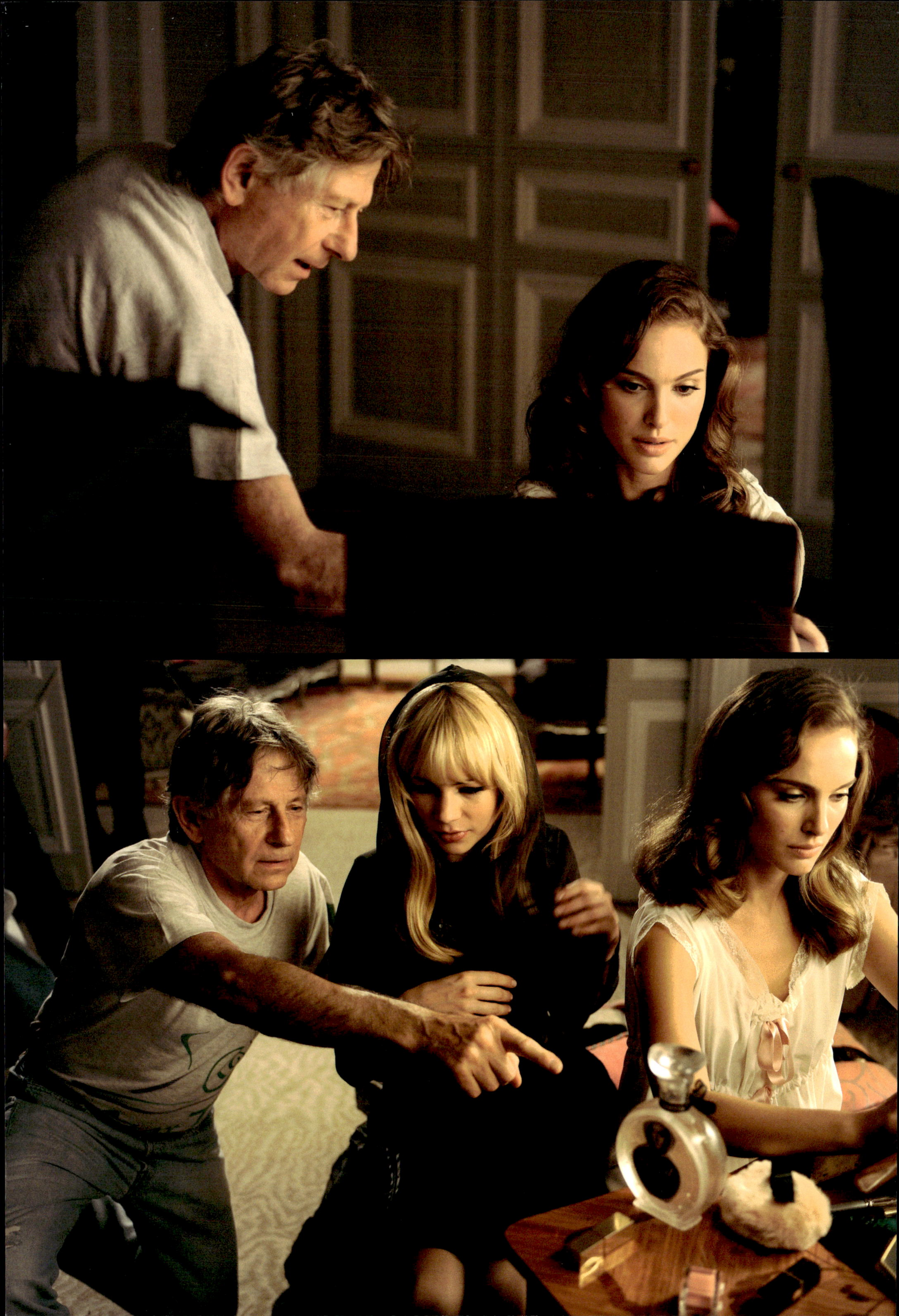

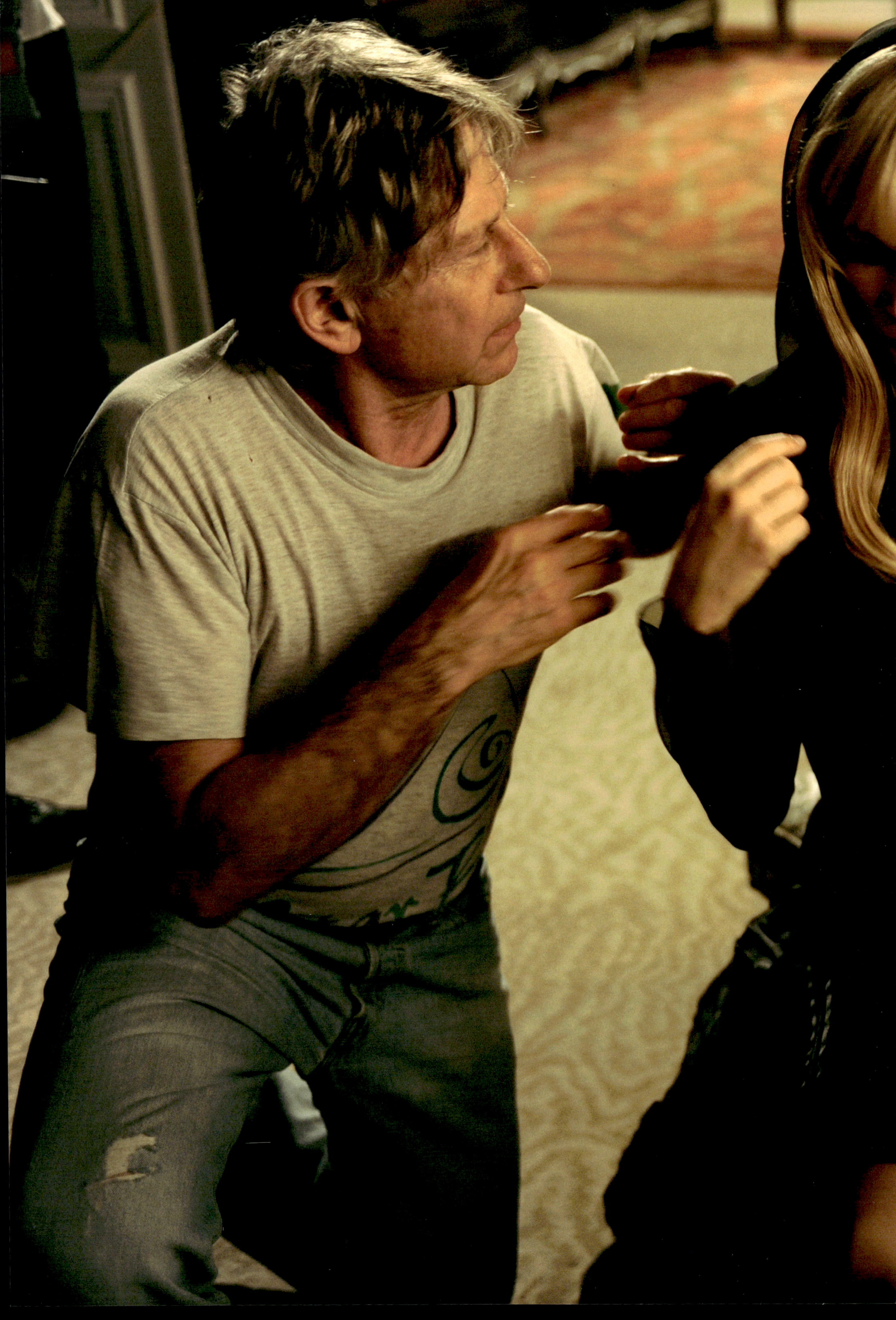

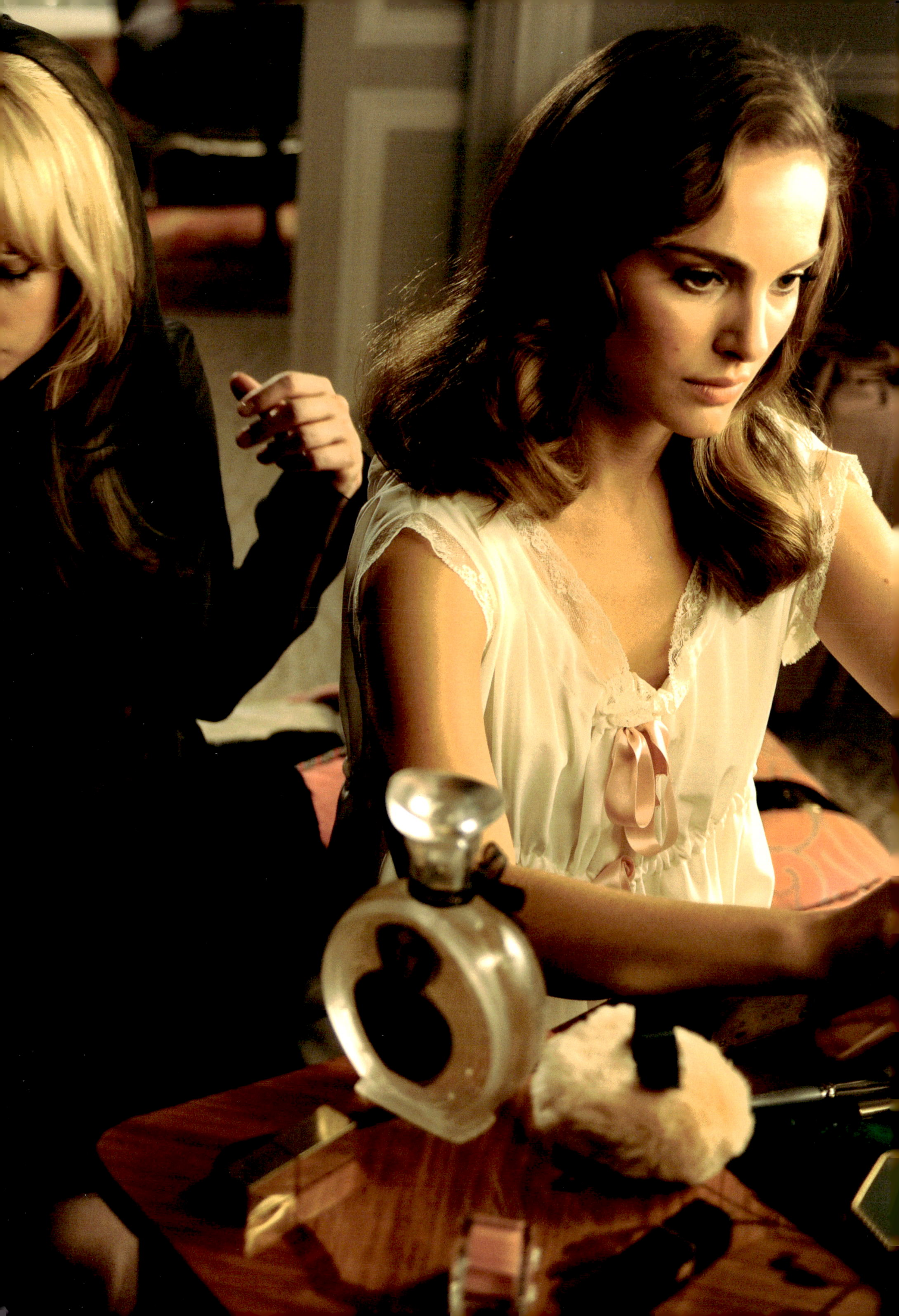

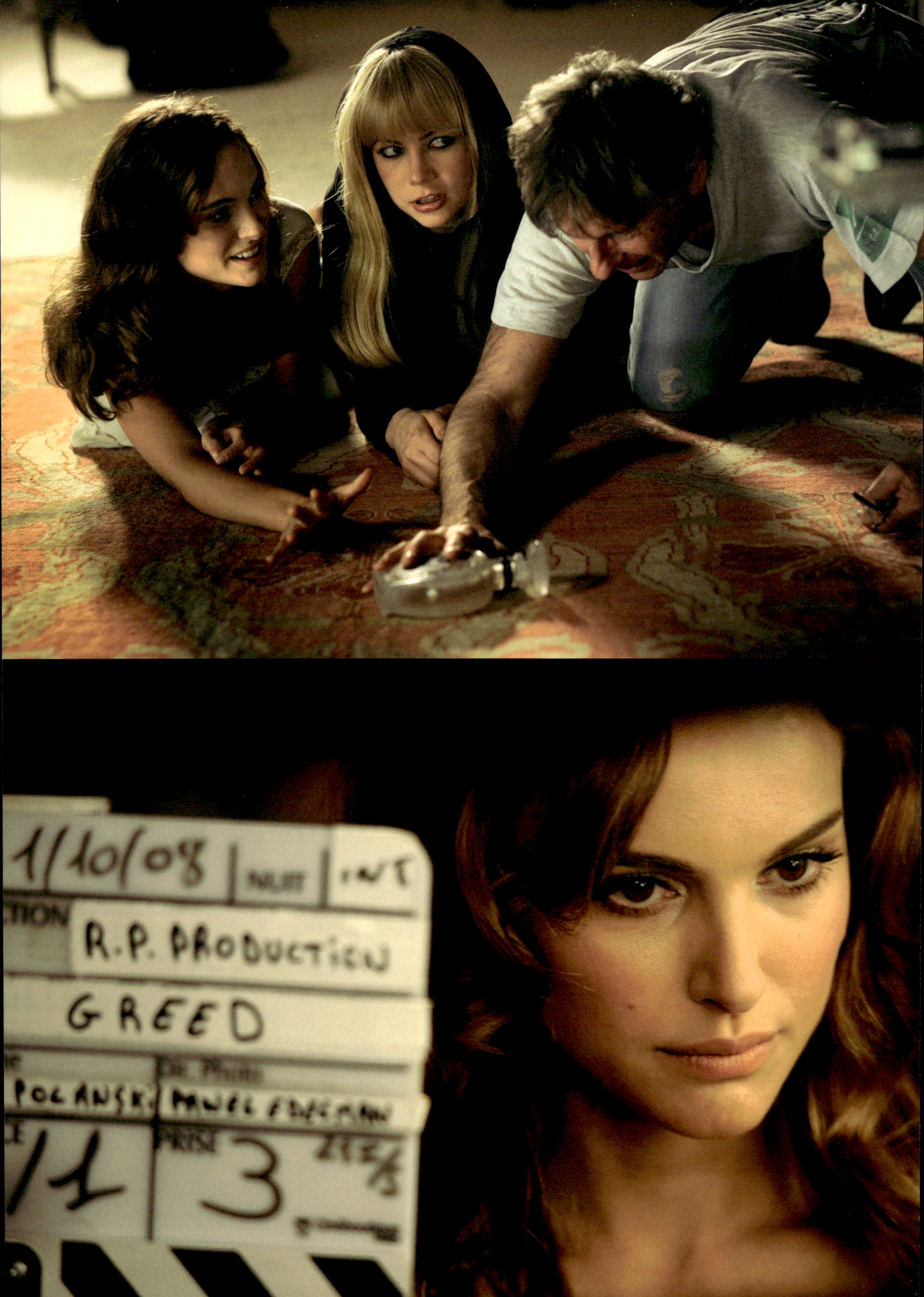

1/10/08
R.P. PRODUCTION
GREED
POLANSKI
3

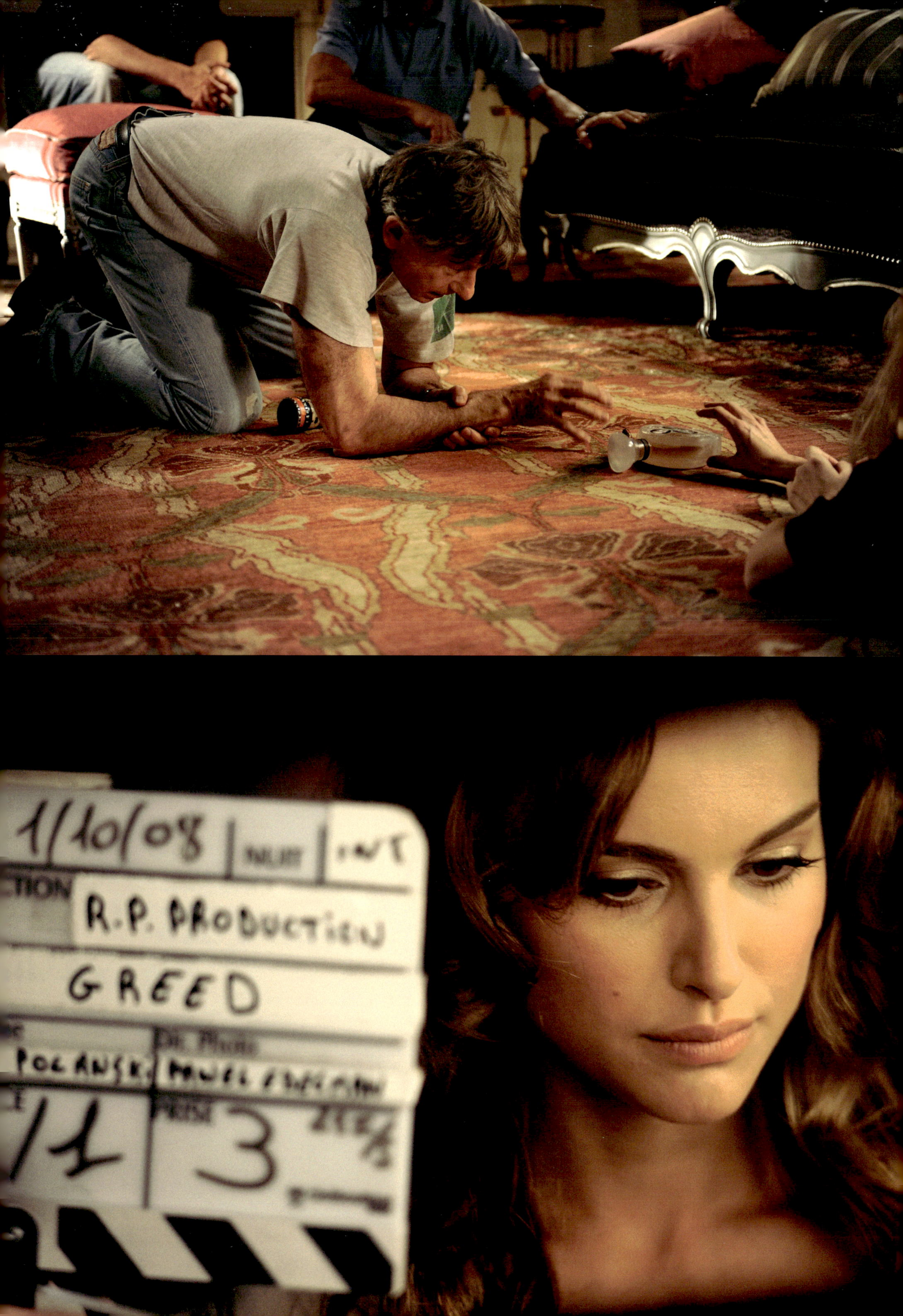
1/10/08
R.P. PRODUCTION
GREED
POLANSKI
3

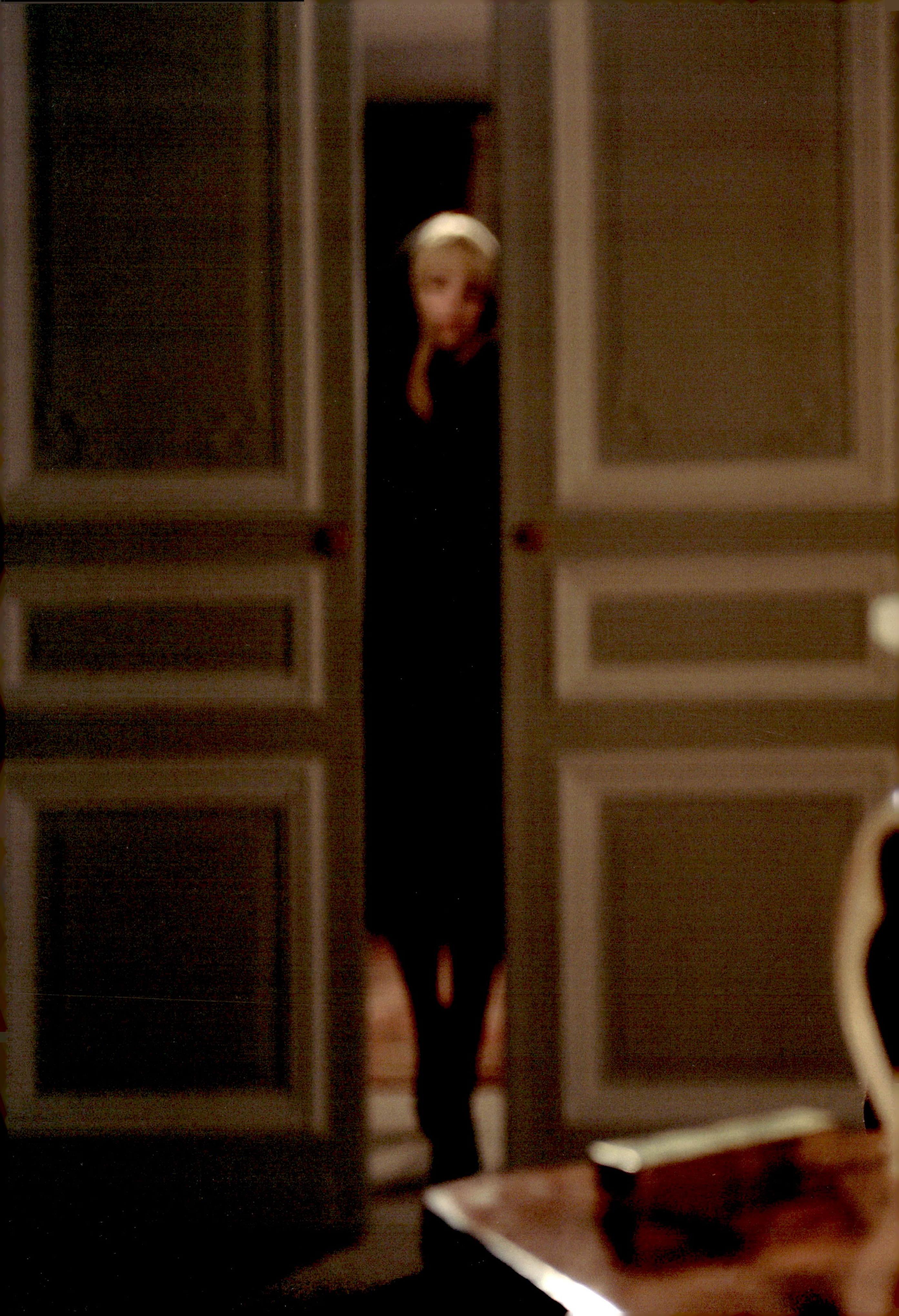

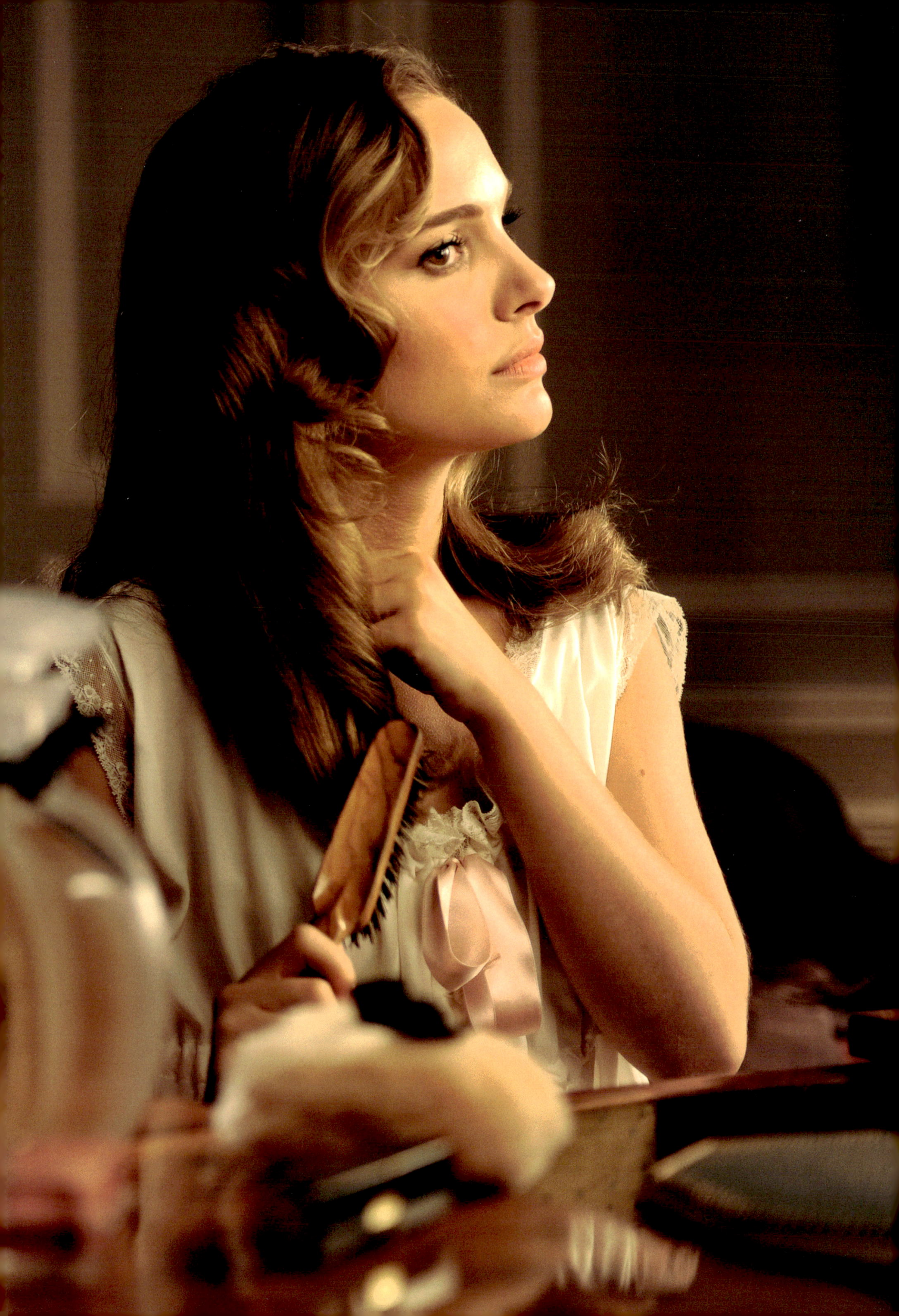

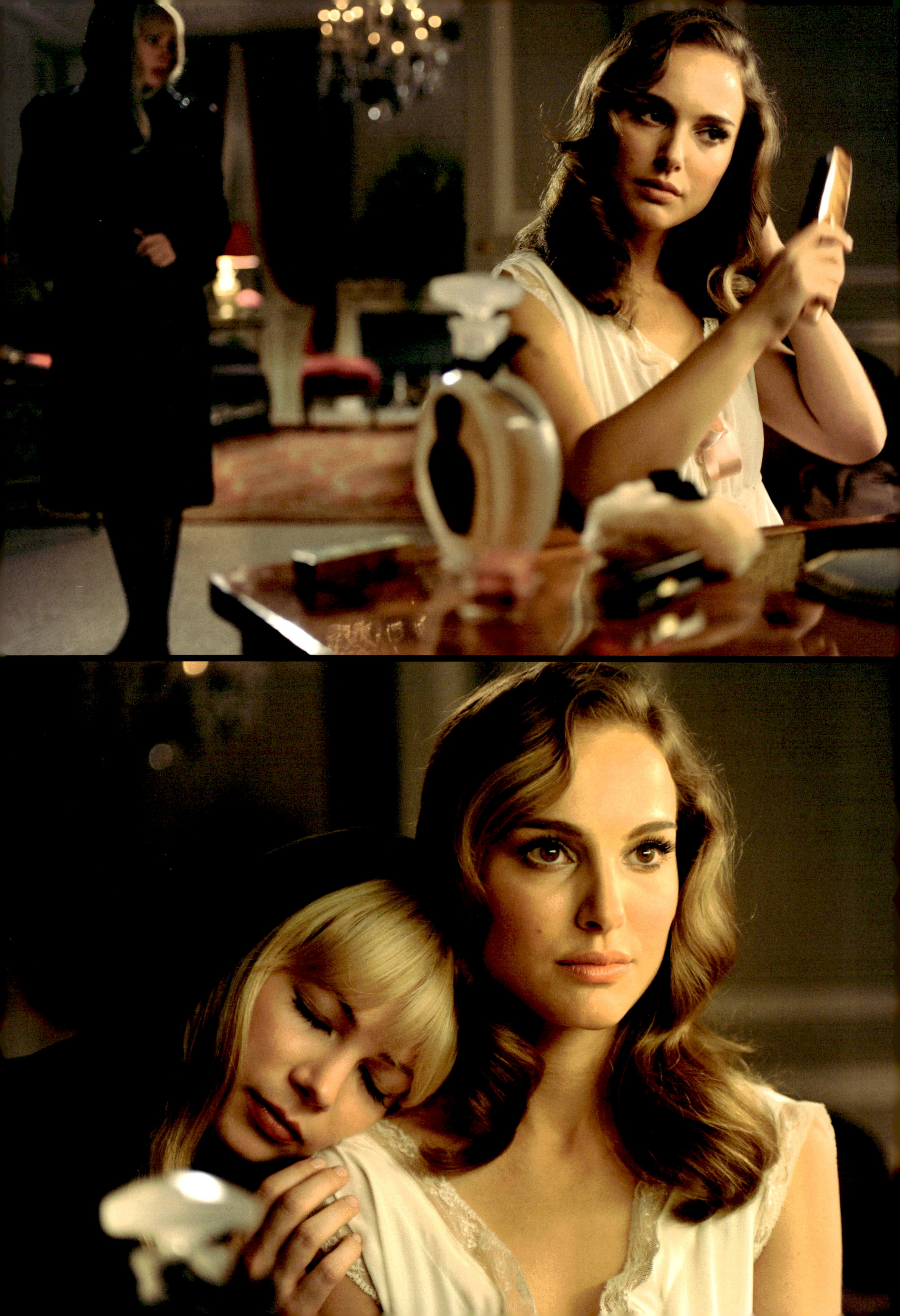

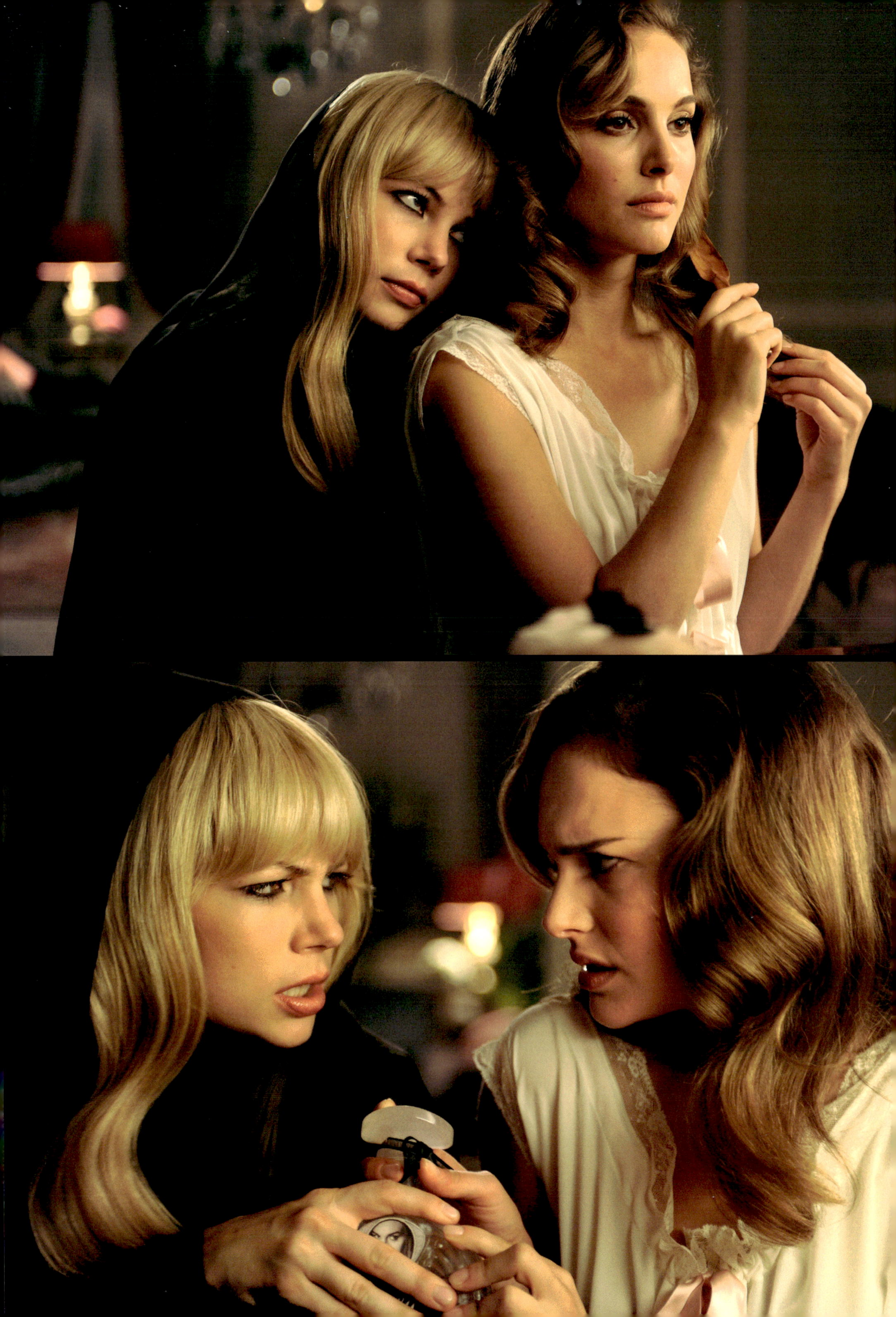

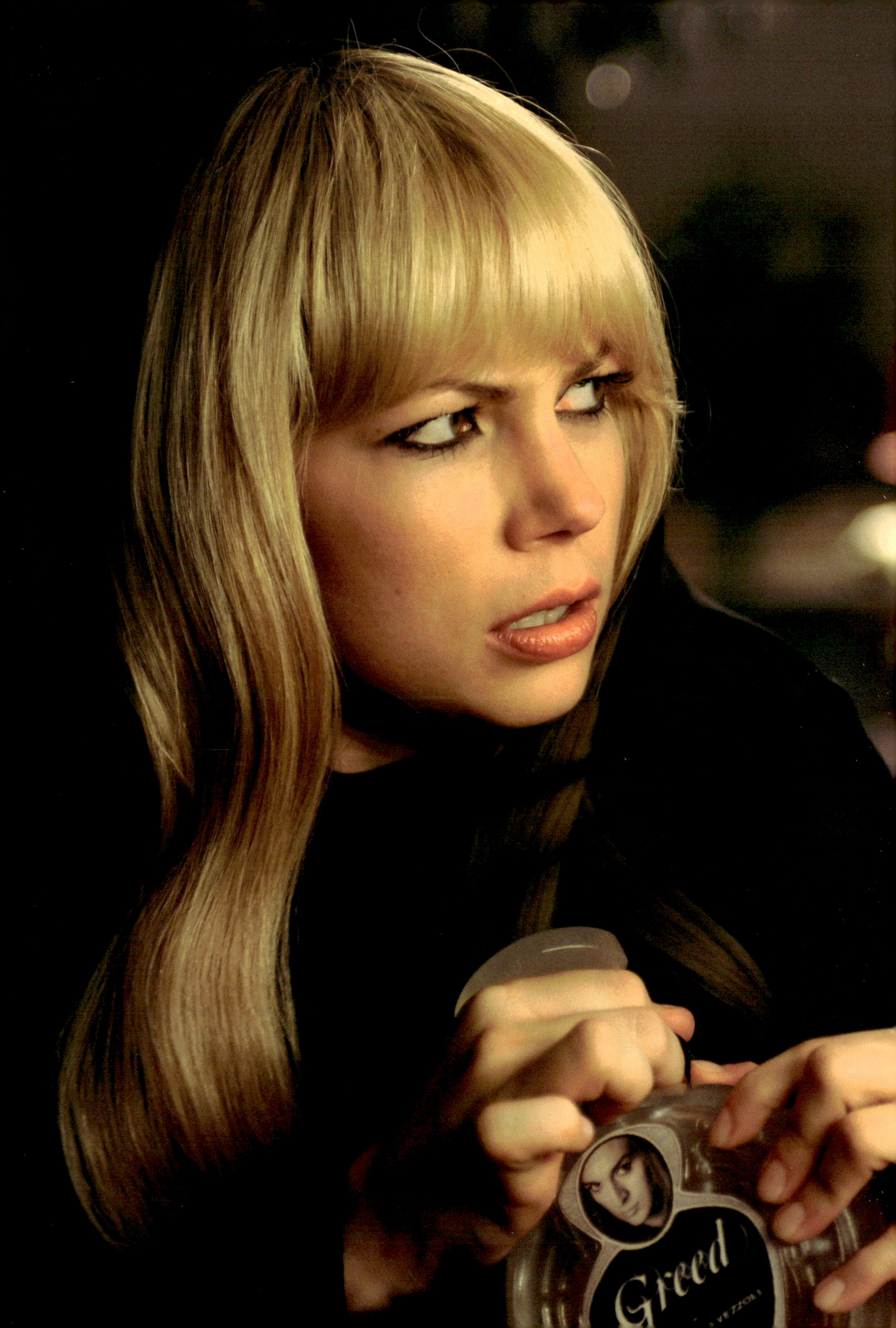

Greed

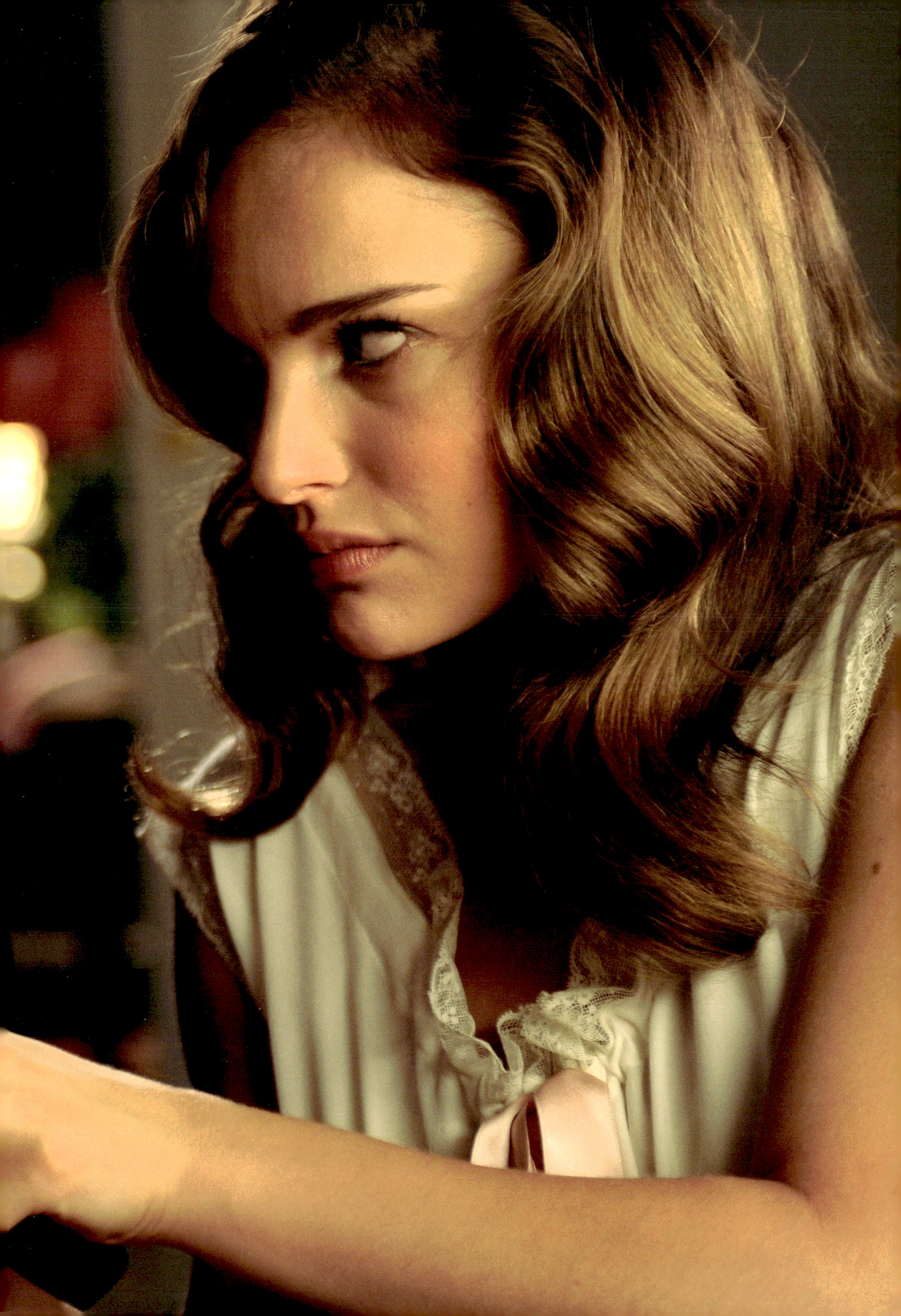

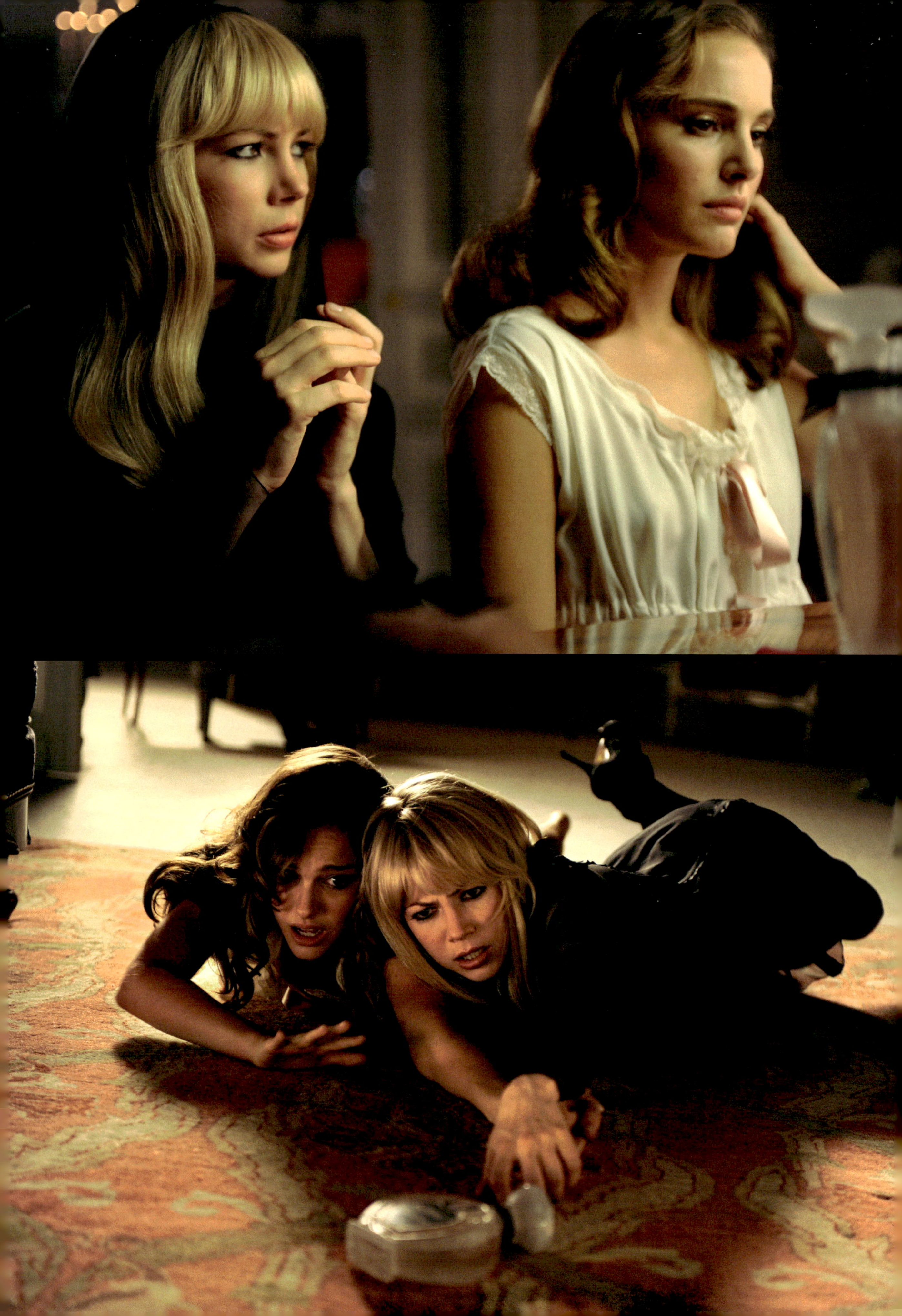

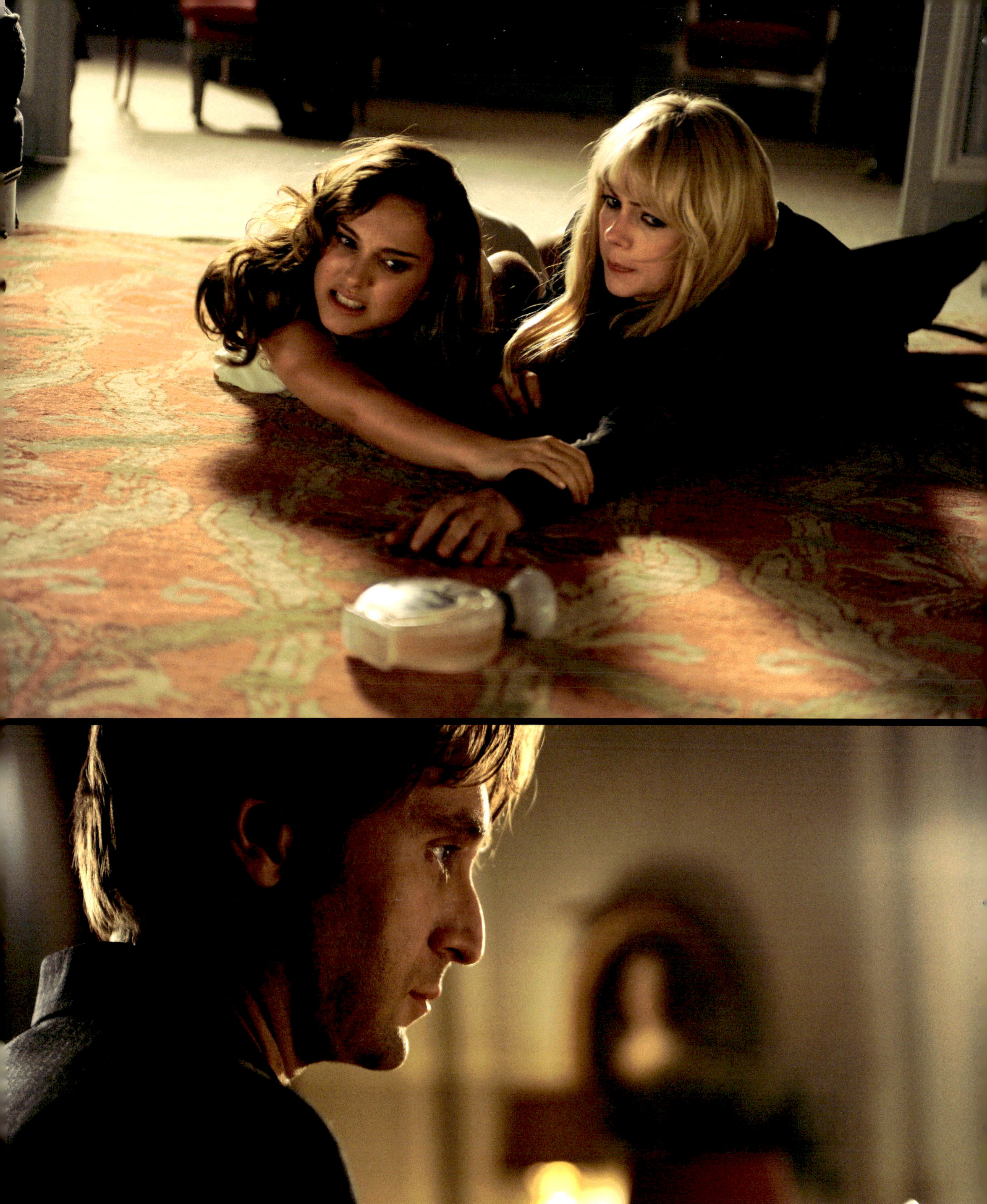

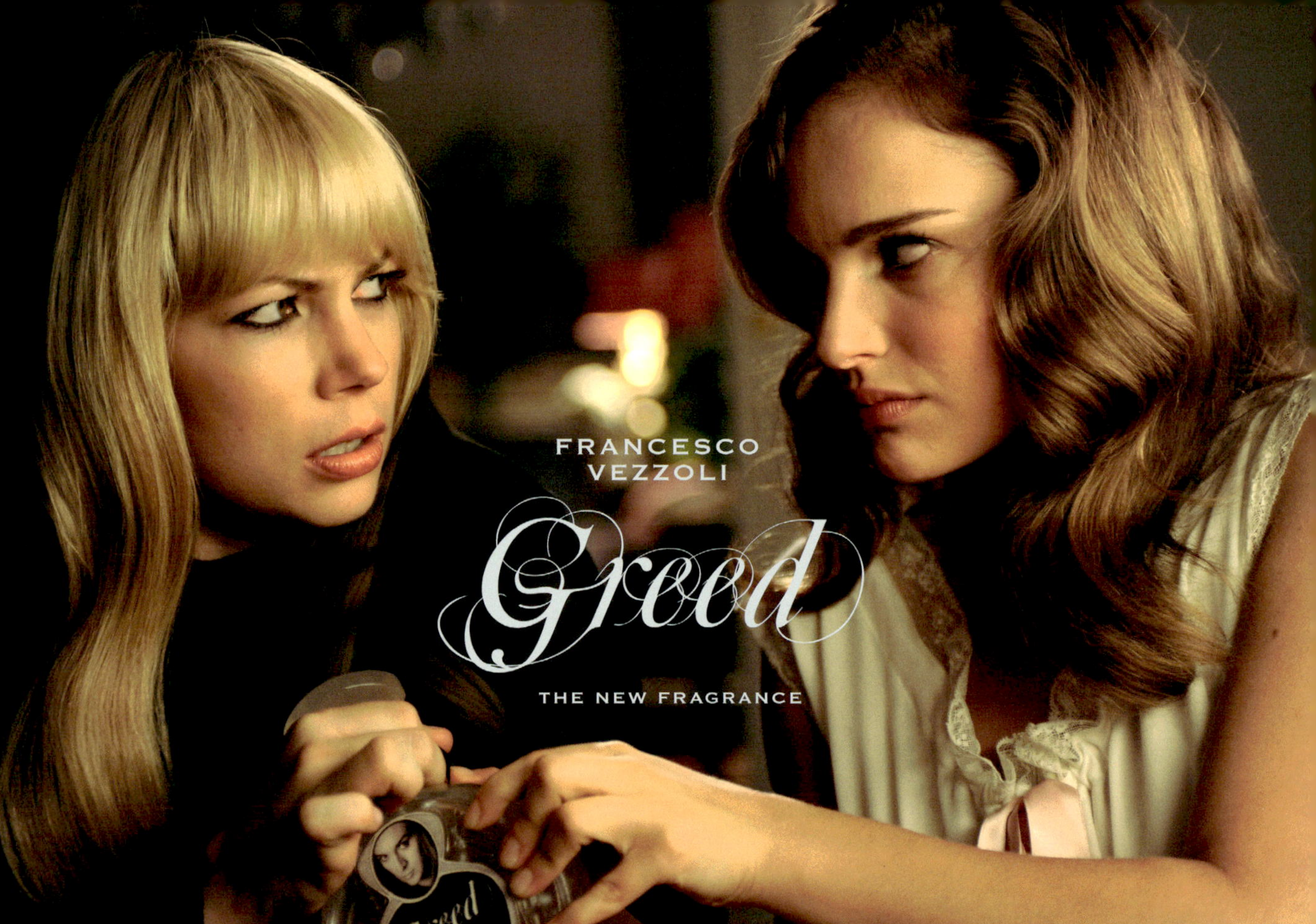

FRANCESCO
VEZZOLI

Greed

THE NEW FRAGRANCE

Greed

Self-Portrait of Francesco Vezzoli
as Produced by Allan Carr
By Bruce Hainley

Allan Carr, the producer behind the popular movie musical *Grease*, the less popular *Grease 2,* and the Tony Award-winning Broadway hit *La Cage aux Folles*, died on Tuesday at his home in Beverly Hills, California. He was sixty-two and also had a home in Palm Springs. He was once called the greatest host since Perle Mesta.

The cause was liver cancer, said Ronni Chasen, a longtime friend.

In a varied career that included stints as a publicist and manager, Mr. Carr was noted for his shrewd timing and keen nose for new talent. He was perhaps just as renowned for his penchant for camp, most notably as the producer of the 1989 Academy Awards telecast, which came to be regarded as the most vulgar presentation ever. Mr. Carr rechristened the Shrine Exhibition Hall's greenroom as the elaborate "Club Oscar," and changed the award announcement to "And the Oscar goes to . . ." With production pointers from *Beach Blanket Babylon,* that show's opening number included a duet between the actor Rob Lowe and a pipsqueak Snow White (butchering a razzle-dazzle rewrite of the Ike and Tina Turner song "Proud Mary" and prompting legal action by the Walt Disney company); dancing cocktail tables; a high-kicking chorus line of movie-theater usherettes; and Merv Griffin singing "I've Got a Lovely Bunch of Coconuts" to an audience of legendary stars—Doris Day, Dorothy Lamour, Cyd Charisse, Vincent Price—sprinkled across the stage like pearls among mothballs. It lasted an agonizing twelve minutes.

Reared in Highland Park, Illinois, he was born Alan Solomon, an only child, to Albert and Ann Solomon, on May 27, 1937, a Gemini. "The Gemini personality is all or nothing" Mr. Carr once provided. "I tried nothing once for four weeks in Hawaii. My mind turned to mai tais." Mr. Carr attended Lake Forest College and entered show business after studying briefly at Northwestern University. With a "friend," he invented the concept for the *Playboy* television series, which helped pave the way for Hugh Heffner's Playboy clubs. "Most people don't realize that the clubs came *after*—they were an offshoot of this television show that we created in Chicago," Mr. Carr related about his big start. "The first show had Ella Fitzgerald and Lenny Bruce. We had one big star, then a newcomer and then an East Side act—people who had not yet been on television. It was Bobby Short's first time on television, Mable Mercer's, Frances Faye's—people from the Blue Angel and the Bon Soir and the Carlyle . . ." He was also responsible for the opening of the Civic Theater in Chicago, where he underwrote *The World of Carl Sandburg* with Bette Davis and Gary Merrill. "We were leaving the theater one night," he relished telling, "and Bette goes into the closet and takes out this really ratty mink coat. 'I got this in 1950, the same year I got Gary. That was ten years ago. Do you know what? The coat's held up better.' And Gary turns to her and says: 'The coat gets less abuse.' And that's the way they were when they were married . . . it was just like they were living *All About Eve*."

With a string of minor films under his belt, including *The First Time* in 1969 with Jacqueline Bisset, a last minute replacement for Leslie Caron, he bought a Tudor mansion in the Benedict Canyon. The fifteen-room house had been the pad of a succession of luminaries. "Do you know who lived here?" he thrilled. "Ingrid Bergman! Imagine! Later, director Richard Quine bought the house to entertain Kim Novak, planted lavender flowers, installed a mirror over the bed and built secret closets." Mr. Carr kept his collection of five-dozen caftans, Japanese kimonos, and velvet and satin suits within. The living room was three storeys high, large enough to play basketball in, which is what actor James Caan, the tenant before Carr, did. The bedroom once occupied by Bergman's daughter, Pia Lindstrom, was a guest room and remained much the way she had it as a child, all chintz and ruffles. The young men who lived or worked at the mansion, Hilhaven, occupied the other bedrooms. It was here, in an atmosphere reeking of good dope and wine, that Mr. Carr, frequently in full *Ah Men* catalog splendor, wearing an animal-printed silky jumpsuit or caftan, would knit the plans for the infamous Wednesday night parties he hosted. Liza Minnelli, Rudolph Nureyev, Bette Midler, and assorted young things were all known to have had a good time with Carr, who would often be joined by one of his new finds, like hunky young Tim Sullivan, making himself right at home.

Mr. Carr brought *Survive!* to Robert Stigwood in 1975. Based on *Superviventes de los Andes*, a Mexican potboiler about the true-life ordeal of sixteen Uruguayan soccer players who survived a plane crash in the snowbound Andes for ten weeks by eating the bodies of their dead teammates, Carr dubbed in some dreary English dialogue, added a few scenes, and exploited the film with his considerable talent and the backing of Paramount. Many in Hollywood deplored *Survive!* as a vulgar rip-off, but it made a $13 million profit. "It was not a good movie," Carr once shrugged, "but I think the eating scenes were tasteful."

Mr. Carr went on to produce *Grease*, the 1978 teenage dance extravaganza starring John Travolta and Olivia Newton-John. True to form, he took a chance on two relative newcomers to the industry: Mr. Travolta had yet to appear in *Saturday Night Live*, as the *New York Times*, in an obit for Mr. Carr, erroneously titled *Saturday Night Fever*, and Ms. Newton-John, a singer who "knocked out" Mr. Carr when he met her at a party, had appeared only once before the camera, in *Toomorrow*, a British flop. *Grease* became one of the highest-grossing films in history.

Known as the Elsa Maxwell of Hollywood and as what *Women's Wear Daily* dubbed "a Busby Berkeley mini-extravaganza sporting Gucci loafers and the fastest mouth this side of The Bistro," Mr. Carr threw parties gilding his reputation for making "fantasies come true." At Hilhaven, he threw a shindig he described as "the Cannes Festival moved to Beverly Hills" in the summer of 1975. Everyone from A to Z—meaning from the "A" Irving Lazars, Jennings Langs, and Henry Mancinis to what the "Z's" Rex Reed referred to as "a bunch of hustlers from Hollywood and Santa Monica Blvds., in particular Kyle, Brick, Anthony #4, Chad, and one guy going by the sonorous handle of Beercan." Some of the boys sported T-shirts reading "Amyl Nitrate," and stories about the goings-on ran rampant—that all the bedrooms were locked, and someone overdosed on the front lawn in a pile of beer cans, causing the arrival of the police. "I have no front lawn," Carr averred. "I checked. What happened was a crasher collapsed on my neighbor's lawn. Only two bedrooms were locked, one where the servants change and one where the Cycle Sluts were getting dressed. Liza, Lorna, and Alto were helping them get made up." Male guests skinny-dipped in the pool. One all-American TV sweetheart was heard muttering: "I've lost the keys to my life, the keys to my house, my car, my *everything*."

Mr. Carr threw his two-night "Rolodex" soirée—"Rolodex" because guests were invited alphabetically in two groups, A to L on the first night, the rest of the alphabet on the second—to warm his Malibu home. The host changed his clothes, all by La Vetta and including a scarf caftan, a Japanese obi jacket with harem pants, and an Egyptian fisherman's tunic and pants, three times during each party. The gold-and-lapis jewelry chosen to accessorize each change had been designed by Dale Rosenstock of Medici.

At his party-giving zenith, Mr. Carr built a private disco, rumored to have been designed and decorated by Cher, in an old rehearsal hall in his basement. The resulting flamboyant opulence—done in an Egyptian motif complete with metallic copper banquettes, satin pillows galore, a copper floor with running lights that moved with the rhythm of the music; mirrors that reflected to infinity; copper-and-gold palm trees, and various Egyptian artifacts (both originals and copies)—took nine months to complete. There were copper plaques to mark reserved seats for Carr and friends Regine, Steve Rubell, and Scott Forbes. A somewhat de trop neon sign proclaimed ALLAN CARR'S DISCO and another glowed in memory of failed Zanuck star Bella Darvi.

Failing numerous attempts with SlimFast, and having tried every diet ever invented, from a Brazilian "sleep" diet inducing the subject into coma to the Andy Warhol diet ("Andy told me you should always order what you like least on the menu. Then you just taste from everybody else's plate."), Mr. Carr had his jaw wired shut so he wouldn't be able to eat solids soon after *New York* magazine reported the following on his ballooning weight: "There was Allan Carr, relaxing on the beach in Barbados and drawing stares for his red-, white-, and blue-striped caftan. Suddenly, from nowhere, came a huge wave that gathered up the portly producer and his deck chair and sent them tumbling down the beach. Carr was left like a beached great white whale, quite naked. The delighted tourists snapped pictures of his predicament until Carr untangled himself, blushing, and fled to his yacht." Starved, he later announced he was "thin enough to wear Madras again" and to celebrate he acquired a triplex on Central Park South—called Viewhaven, in keeping with his luxe villa in Hawaii, Surfhaven, and his Malibu hideaway, Seahaven—with three terraces, a sauna, and a greenhouse in the sky.

Life was an Allan Carr production, as he once explained in a blow-by-blow of his type "A" personality: "I take responsibility for the details— clothes, hair, makeup, locations; the look and feel of the films, of everything, are mine . . . Naturally a lot of people in Hollywood, the ones who trade in mediocrity, think I'm crazy. I've worked damned hard to get here. I mean, when I'm working on a picture, it's mine, and I get up at six o'clock . . . and . . . my only respite many mornings are those moments, mine, when I sit on the toilet, reading my mail and *The Hollywood*

Reporter. It's not attractive, but it happens to be my favorite morning activity, mine. Every day brings a whole new mountain of details, most of which are pretty mundane but mine nevertheless. I keep two secretaries with me and issue a list of instructions each morning. Today's agenda was typical: Arrange for tickets to Gilda Radner's show and find out if Gilda wants to eat at Wally's or Elaine's or not at all; Valerie Perrine's birthday is coming up, so call Cake and Art and have a reproduction of her face made in a cake; send my beige pants to be pressed; have my roller skates stretched, 'cause I can't get my feet in them; tell Halston I feel terrible, but I can't stay in town for Liza's opening. That kind of stuff ..."

Although Mr. Carr was noted for discovering Michelle Pfeiffer, Mark Hamill, Steve Guttenberg, Lisa Hartman, and Miles O'Keefe, while also guiding and enhancing the careers of Ann-Margret, Peter Sellers, Melina Mercouri, Frankie Valli, Herb Alpert & The Tijuana Brass, Petula Clark, Joan Rivers, Peggy Lee, Keir Dullea, Rosalind Russell, Tony Curtis, Mama Cass Elliott, Marvin Hamlisch, the German shepherd Won Ton Ton, Paul Anka, Dyan Cannon, Stockard Channing, and Marisa Berenson, little has come to light on how Mr. Carr first spotted Maxwell Caulfield, whom he cast as his male lead in *Grease 2,* although it's assumed it was while Mr. Caulfield starred, Off-Broadway, in the title role of Joe Orton's *Entertaining Mr. Sloane,* murderous, sexy drifter, shirtless in black leather pants; little on whether he was made dizzy by the sight or whether he started to burn, gemlike, with the fever of which Peggy Lee murmured. Ditto pal Jeff Paul, who helped him supervise tryouts for male dancers in *Discoland,* the working title for what became *Can't Stop the Music,* or lithe Russell Todd, star of Carr's remake of *Where the Boys Are.*

Mr. Carr made his dramatic debut with Angie Dickinson in *Police Woman* for an episode titled "Murder with Pretty People," in which he portrayed a Scavullo-type fashion photographer suspected of murdering the head of a modeling agency, played by Anne Francis. He hired Nancy Walker (aka Rhoda's mother and the Bounty lady) to helm his disco extravaganza, *Can't Stop the Music,* and spearheaded various tie-ins: a Baskin-Robbins ice cream flavor called *Can't Stop the Nuts;* a Fleischmann distillers' *Can't Stop the Music* drink booklet featuring endless combinations of cocktails to mix with milk and other fluids. According to one of the Village People, Randy Jones, Mr. Carr spent three to four days shooting and reshooting the YMCA shower sequence: "It's pretty evident ... it may be the only PG-rated film with full-frontal male nudity."

Never realized or greenlit Carr productions: *Candide*, starring
Elton John; *The Student Prince*, with Ann-Margret and Englebert
Humperdinck; a picture with Ann-Margret and Elizabeth Taylor; a
remake of *How to Marry a Millionaire*, starring Tatum O'Neal, Chastity
Bono, and Amy Carter; *Riviera*, teaming Olivia Newton-John, Shaun
Cassidy, Brooke Shields, and Donna Summer; a "Hitchcock-type" thriller
(circa 1980) with Bette Davis; *Chicago* with Liza Minnelli and Goldie
Hawn; and the life story of Goya as a musical, "kind of like *Evita*," for
Placido Domingo.

Notices of his passing referred to him variously as "larger-than-life"
and "colorful" while personifying the "Showbiz '70s"; mentioned "large-
man caftans" and the black-tie dinner-dance he staged at Los Angeles'
historic Lincoln Heights jail for Truman Capote, where guests were
subpoenaed rather than invited, and fingerprinted at the door. Bart
Mills, in the *Daily Breeze*, was the only writer to comment on Carr's sex
life: "Whether Carr himself was gay, last week's obit writers didn't know
or didn't tell. And I didn't ask. When I met him, he was surrounded by
a coterie of handsome young men in a London hotel room furnished
almost entirely with mirrors."

No immediate family members survive.

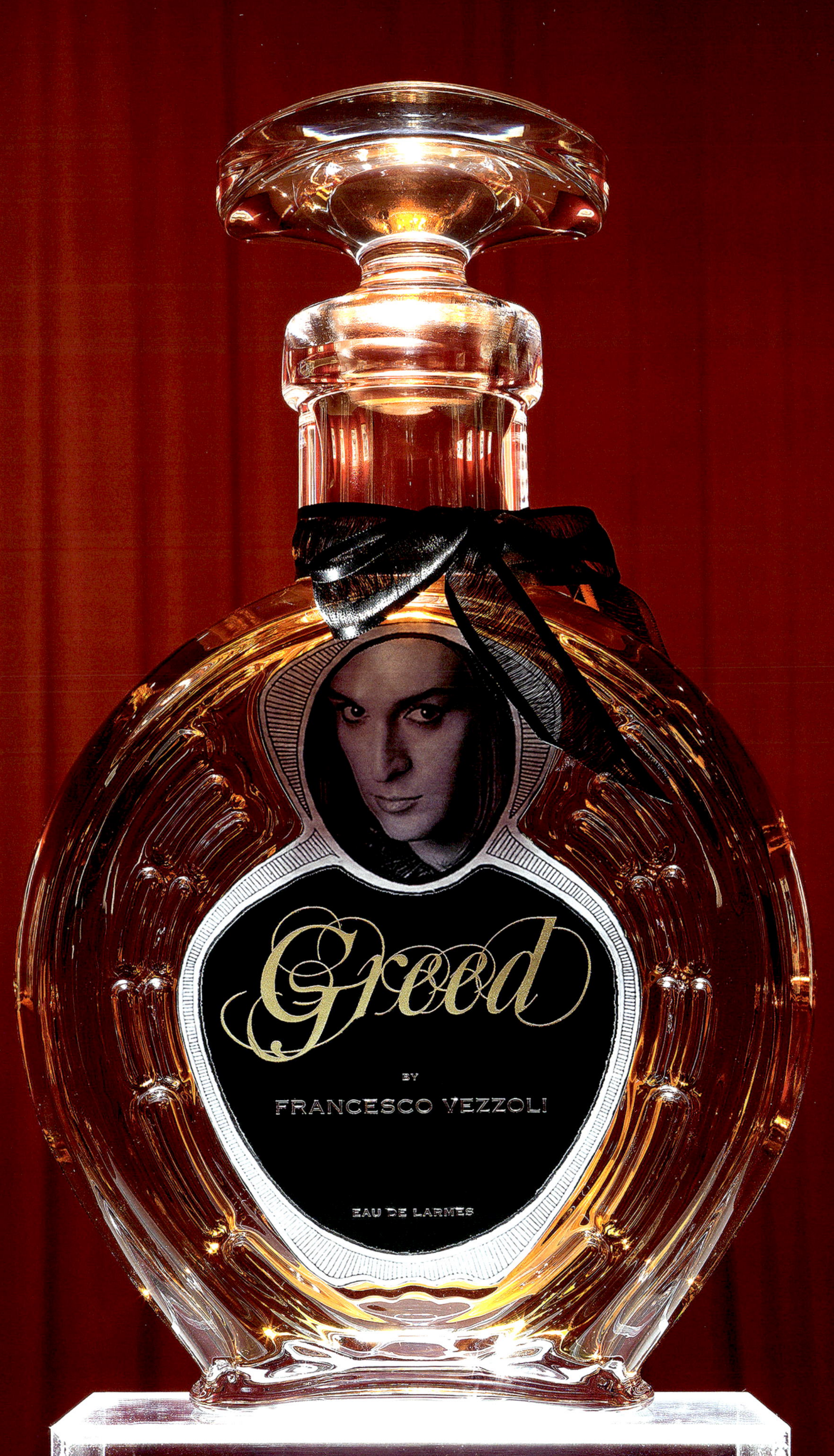
Greed
BY
FRANCESCO VEZZOLI
EAU DE LARMES

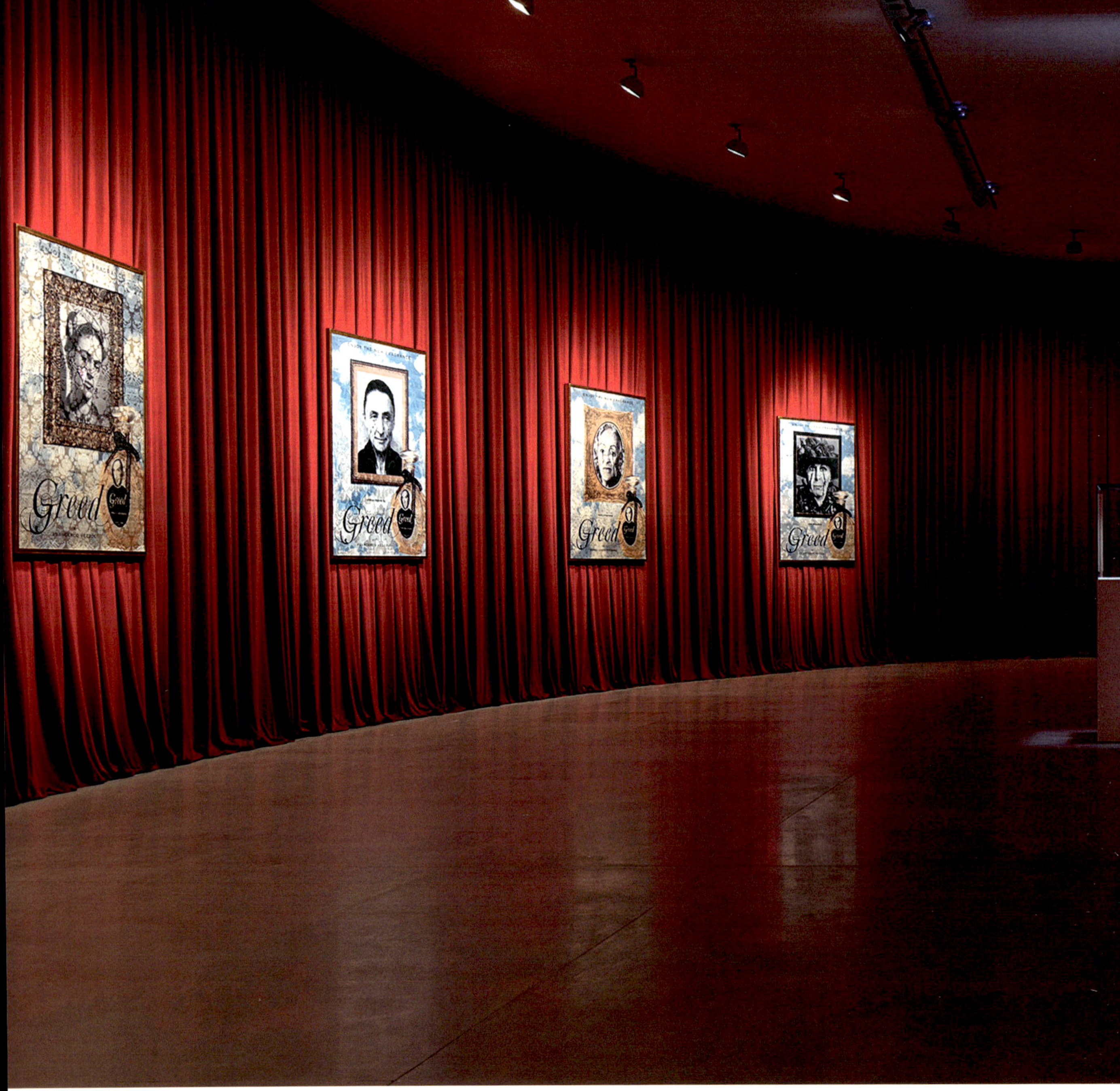

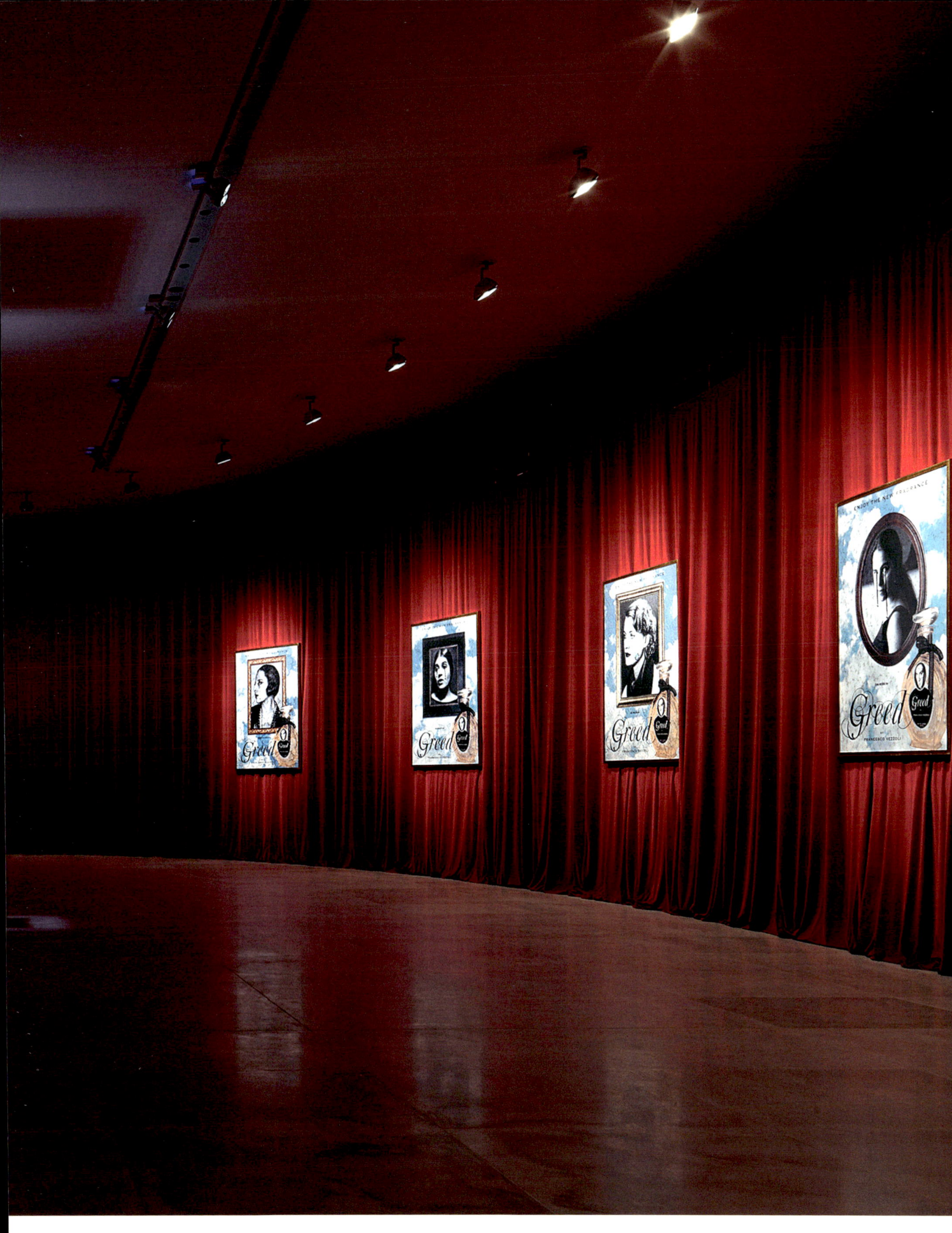
ENJOY THE NEW FRAGRANCE
Greed
Greed
FRANCESCO VEZZOLI

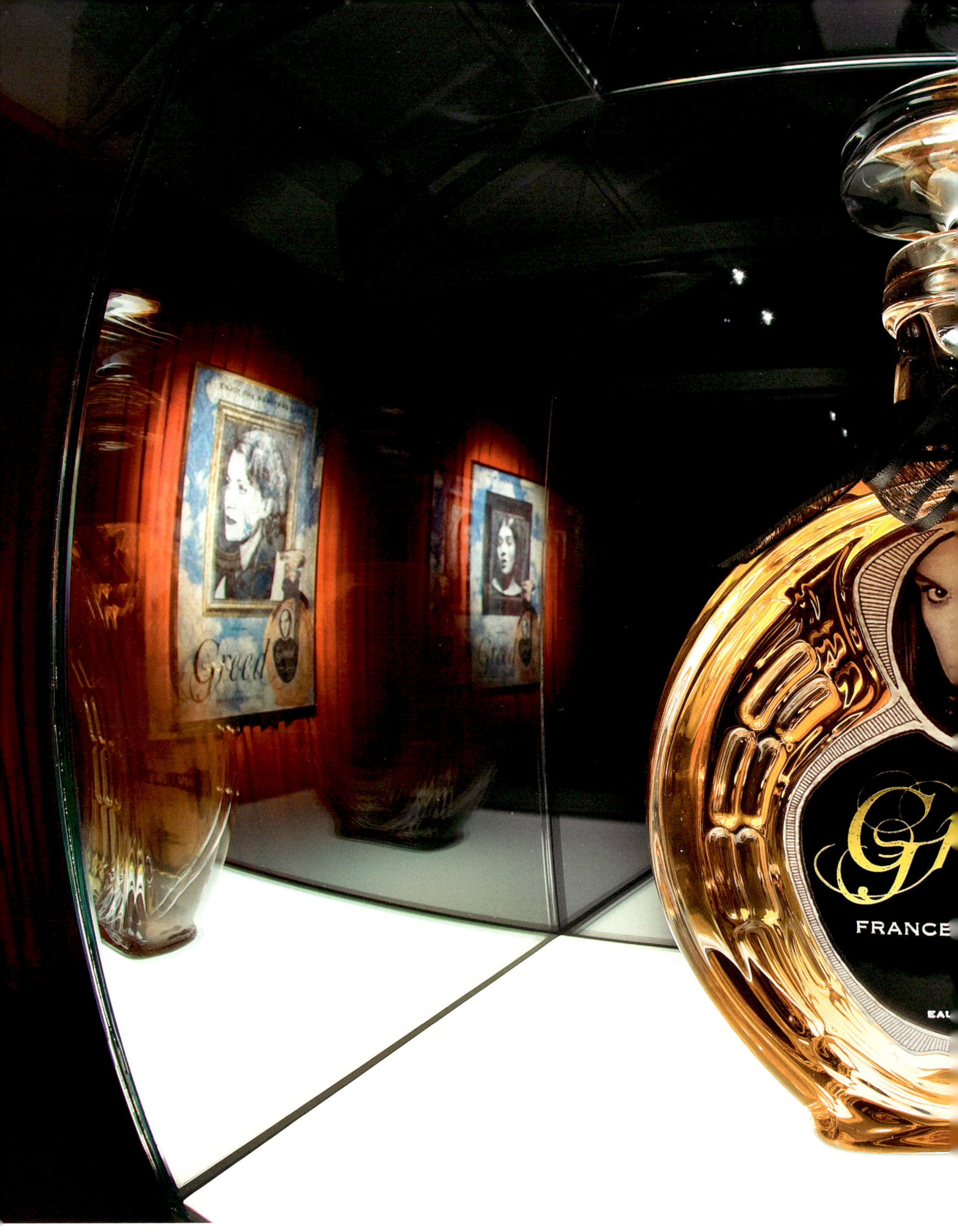

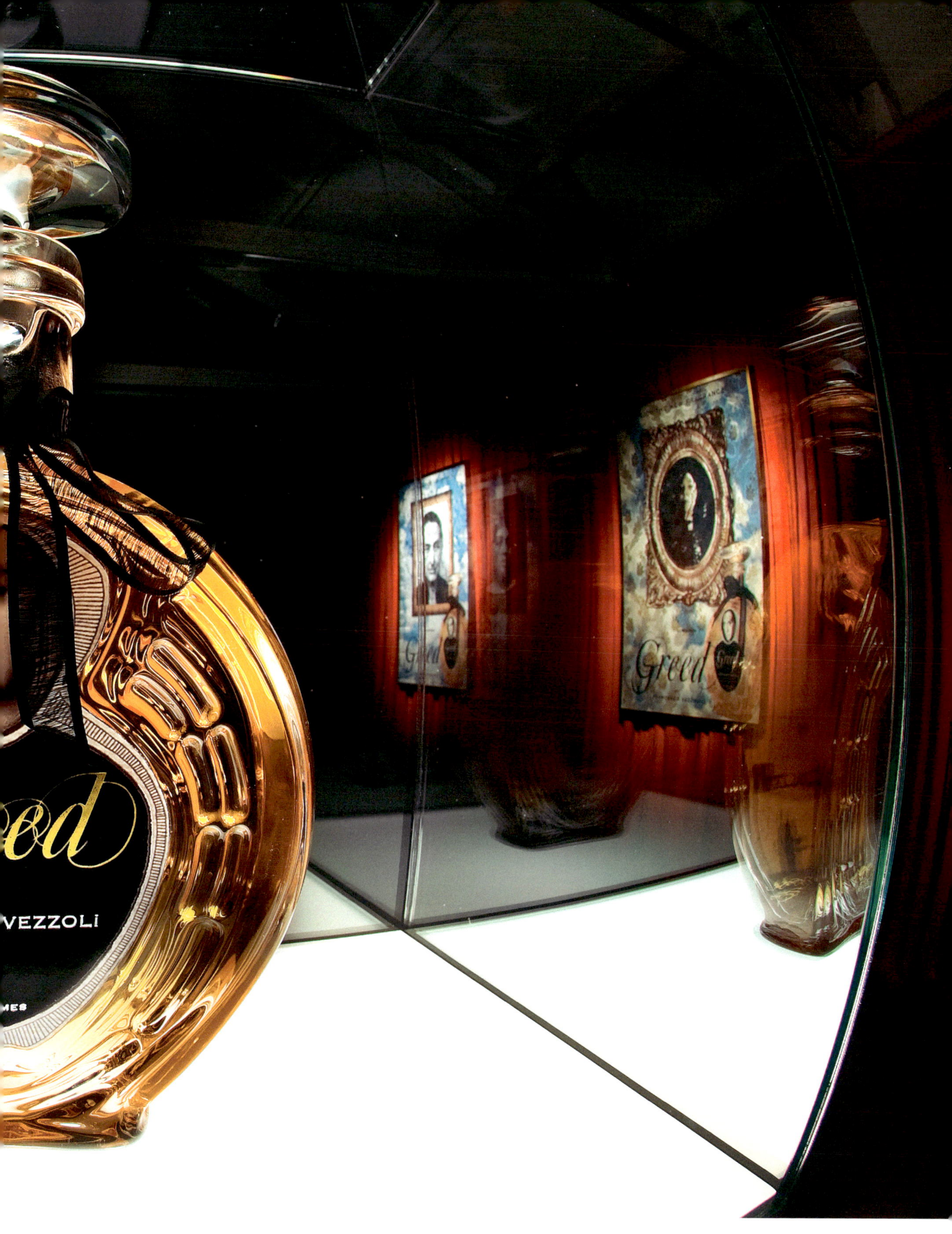

Greed
VEZZOLI
Greed
Greed

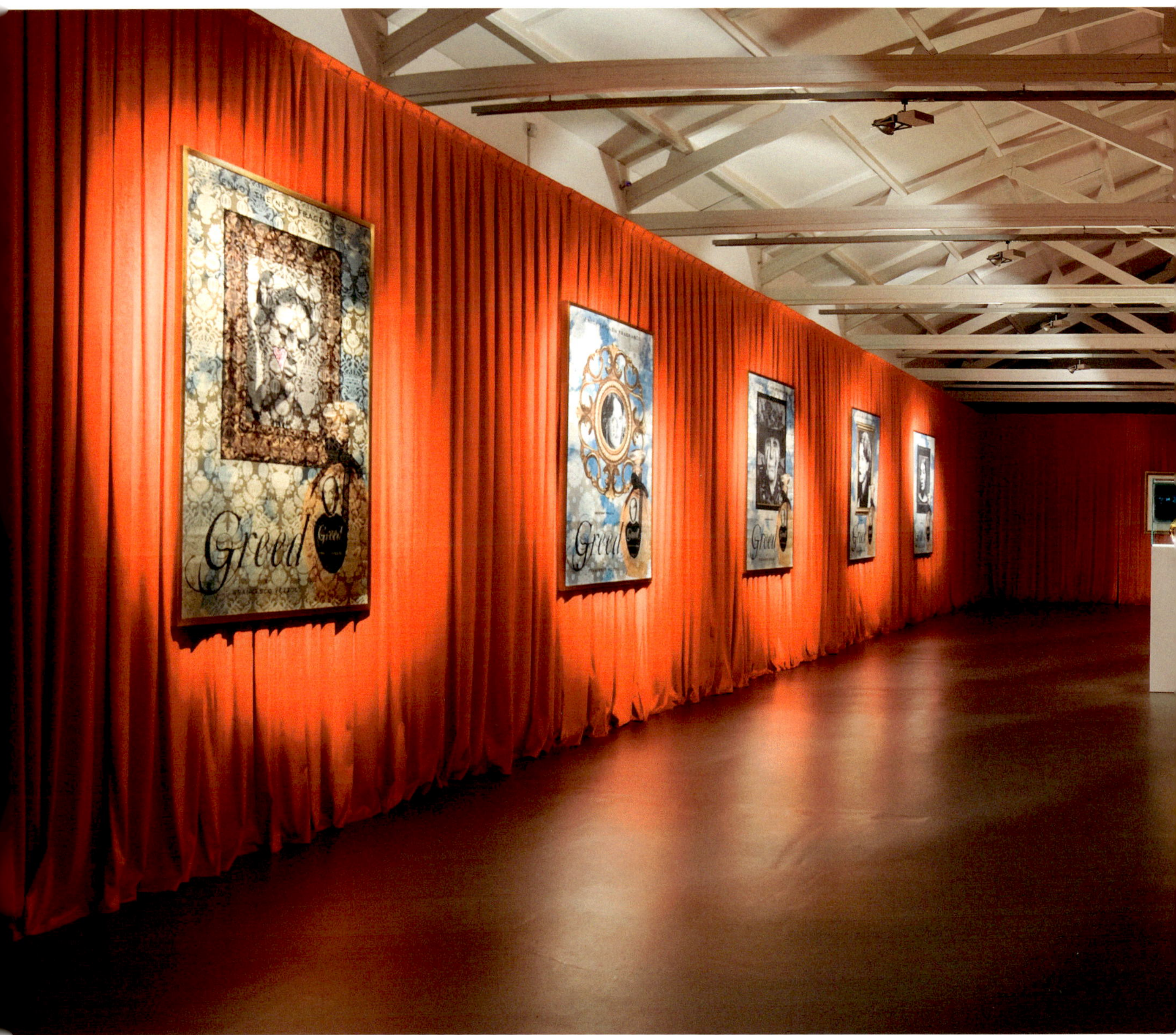

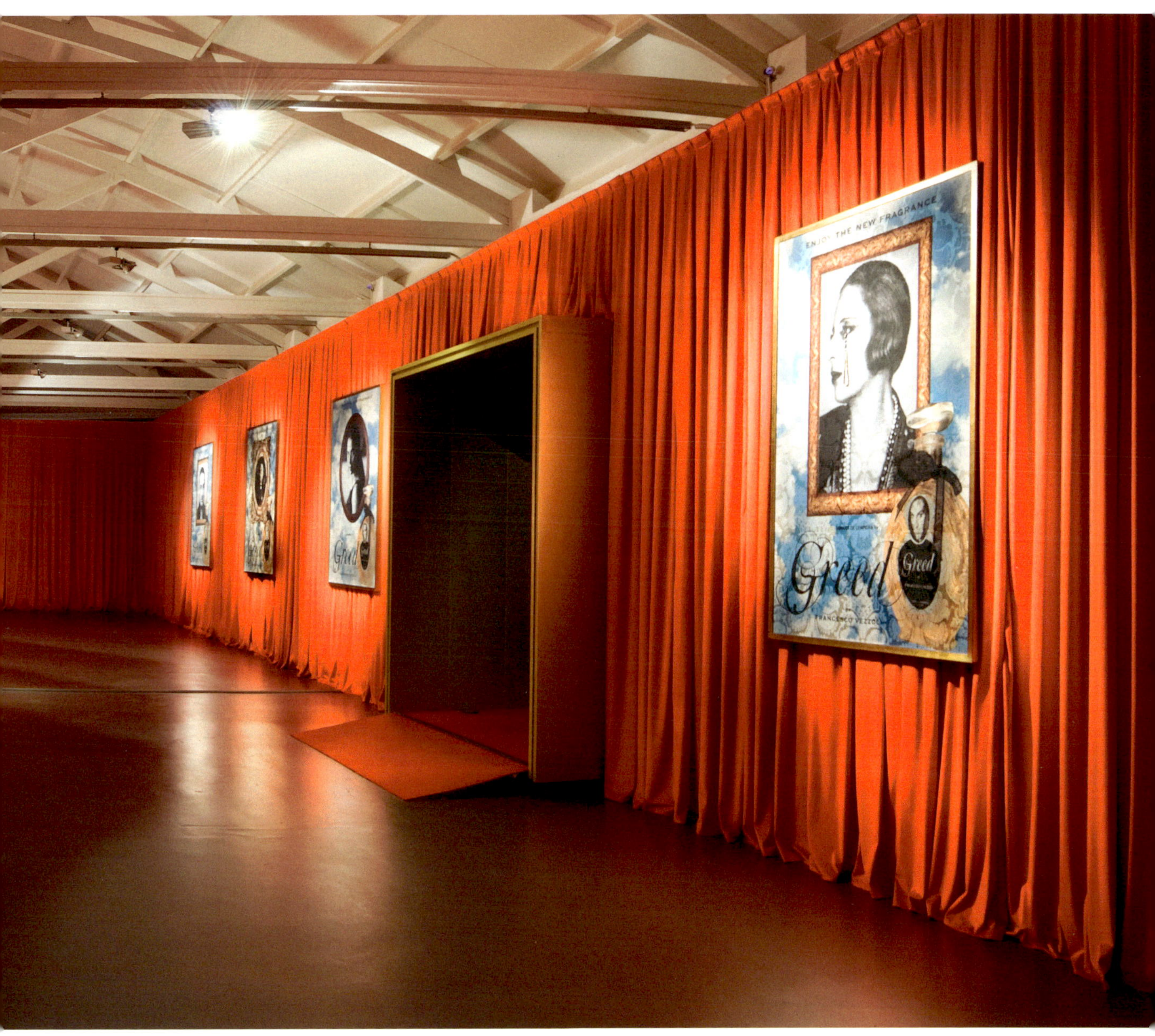

ENJOY THE NEW FRAGRANCE
Greed
Greed
FRANCESCO VEZZOLI

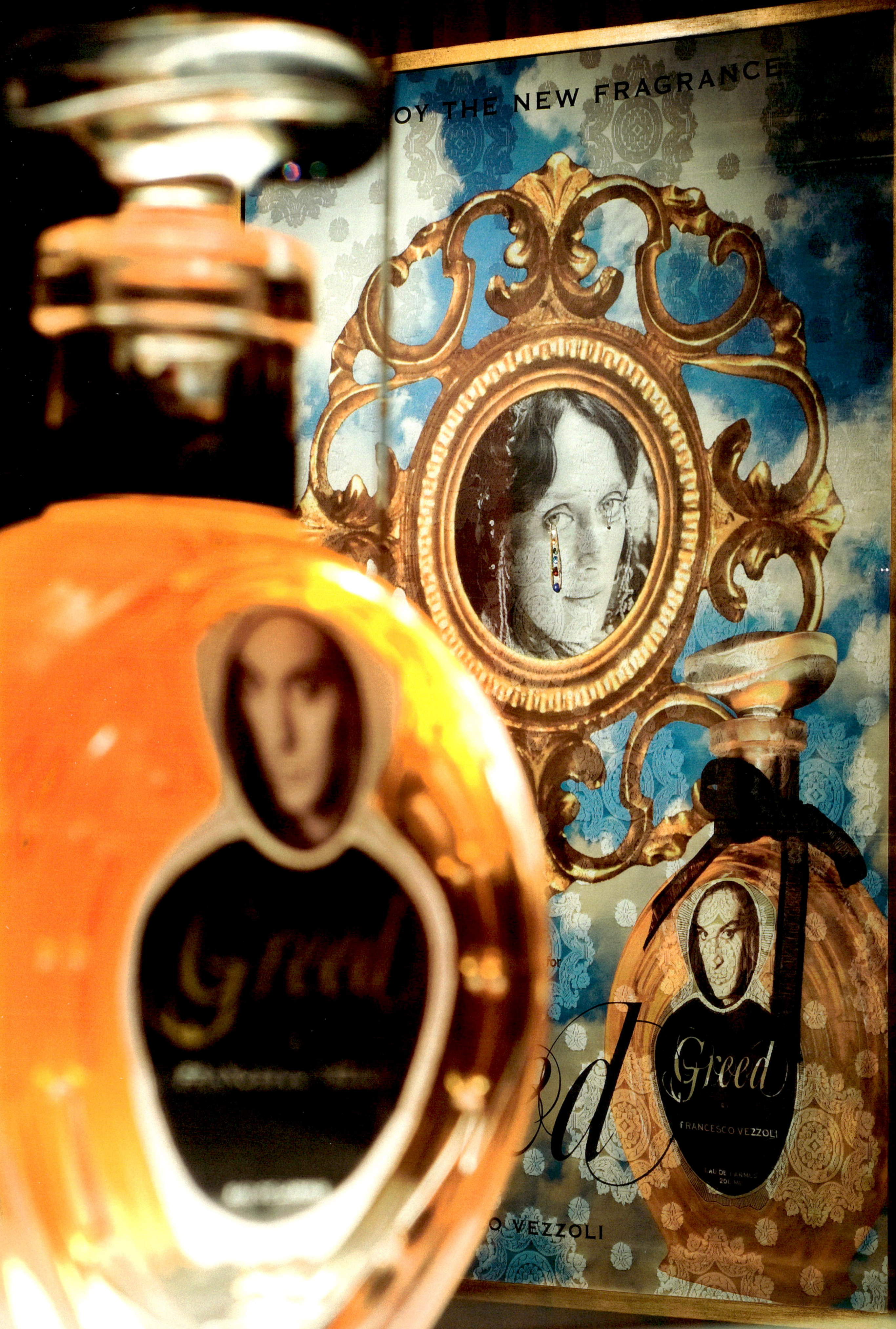
OY THE NEW FRAGRANCE
Greed
Greed
FRANCESCO VEZZOLI
EAU DE LARMES
O VEZZOLI

1971   Born in Brescia, Italy. He lives in Milan.

1992-95   BA, Fine Art, Central St. Martin's School of Art, London.

Solo Shows

2011

- *Sacrilegio*, Gagosian Gallery (W 21st Street), New York
- *Greed, A New Fragrance by Francesco Vezzoli*, La Conservera – Centro de Arte Contemporáneo, Ceutí (Murcia)

2010

- *Francesco Vezzoli: Ballets Russes Italian Style*, The Garage CCC, Moscow

2009

- *Ballets Russes Italian Style (The Shortest Musical You Will Never See Again)*, The MOCA NEW 30th Anniversary Gala, MOCA Museum of Contemporary Art, Los Angeles
- *Francesco Vezzoli: A True Hollywood Story!*, Kunsthalle Wien Project Space, Wien
- *Francesco Vezzoli: A chacun sa vérité*, Galerie Nationale du Jeu de Paume, Paris
- *Dalí Dalí featuring Francesco Vezzoli*, Moderna Museet, Stockholm
- *Greed: A New Fragrance by Francesco Vezzoli*, Gagosian Gallery, Roma

2008

- *Democrazy. An Installation by Francesco Vezzoli*, The Wolfsonian FIU, Miami

2007

- *Francesco Vezzoli: Primadonnas*, Pinakothek der Moderne, München
- *Francesco Vezzoli: A True Hollywood Story!*, The Power Plant, Toronto
- *Right You Are (If You Think You Are)*, Solomon R. Guggenheim Museum, (performance, part of *Performa 07*), New York.
- *Francesco Vezzoli: Democrazy*, Padiglione Italiano, 52ª Esposizione Internazionale d'Arte, La Biennale di Venezia, Venezia
- *Trailer for a Remake of Gore Vidal's Caligula*, Museum Ludwig, Köln

2006
- *Francesco Vezzoli's Caligula*, Museum of Contemporary Art, Beograd
- *Marlene Redux: A True Hollywood Story!*, Tate Modern, London
- *Francesco Vezzoli*, Le Consortium, Dijon
- *The Bruce Nauman Trilogy*, Galerie Neu, Berlin
- *The Gore Vidal Trilogy*, Gagosian Gallery, Beverly Hills

2005
- *Francesco Vezzoli – Trilogia della morte*, Fondazione Cini, Venezia
- *Francesco Vezzoli*, Museu Serralves – Museu de Arte Contemporânea, Porto

2004
- *Premio Acacia 2004*, PAC Padiglione d'Arte Contemporanea, Milano
- *Francesco Vezzoli – Trilogia della morte*, Fondazione Prada, Milano

2002
- *Francesco by Francesco: A Collaboration with Francesco Scavullo*, Galleria Giò Marconi, Milano
- *The Needleworks of Francesco Vezzoli*, Blinky Palermo Award of the East German Savings Bank Foundation for the Free State of Saxony, Galerie für Zeitgenössische Kunst, Leipzig
- *Art Statements* (galleria Giò Marconi, Milano), Art 33 Basel, Basel
- *The Films of Francesco Vezzoli*, New Museum of Contemporary Art, New York
- *Francesco Vezzoli*, Castello di Rivoli Museo d'Arte Contemporanea, Rivoli (Torino)

2000
- *A Love Trilogy – Self-portrait with Marisa Berenson as Edith Piaf*, Spazio Aperto, GAM Galleria Comunale d'Arte Moderna, Bologna

1999
- *Francesco Vezzoli*, Anthony d'Offay Gallery, London
- *An Embroidered Trilogy*, Centre d'Art Contemporain, Genève
- *An Embroidered Trilogy*, GAM Galleria d'Arte Moderna, Bologna (Special Screening)
- *An Embroidered Trilogy*, The British School at Rome, Roma
- *An Embroidered Trilogy*, Galleria Giò Marconi, Milano

2011

• Fondazione Prada at Cà Corner della Regina, Venezia
• *Il mondo vi appartiene – The World Belongs To You*, François Pinault
  Foundation, Palazzo Grassi, Venezia
• *MAXXI Arte / collezione. Il confine evanescente. Immagini italiane dalla
  pittura al digitale*, MAXXI Museo Nazionale delle Arti del XXI secolo, Roma
• *L'insoutenable légèreté de l'être*, Galerie Yvon Lambert, Paris

2010

• *Je crois aux miracles, 10 ans à la Collection Lambert*, Collection Lambert En
  Avignon – Musée d'Art Contemporain, Avignon
• *Cosa fa la mia anima mentre sto lavorando? Opere d'arte contemporanea
  dalla collezione Consolandi*, MAGA Museo Arte Gallarate, Gallarate
  (Varese)
• *Forbidden Love: Art in the Wake of Television Camp*, Kölnischer Kunstverein,
  Köln
• *Contemporary Magic: A Tarot Deck Art Project*, The National Arts Club, New
  York
• *SI – Sindrome Italiana, la jeune création artistique italienne*, Magasin –
  Centre National d'Art Contemporain de Grenoble, Grenoble
• *Che cosa sono le nuvole? Opere dalla collezione Enea Righi*, MUSEION
  Museo d'Arte Moderna e Contemporanea, Bolzano
• *Linguaggi e sperimentazioni. Giovani artisti in una collezione
  contemporanea*, MART Museo d'Arte Moderna e Contemporanea di Trento
  e Rovereto, Rovereto
• *Spazio. Dalle collezioni di arte e architettura del MAXXI*, MAXXI Museo
  Nazionale delle Arti del XXI secolo, Roma

2009

• *The Art of Fashion*, Museum Boijmans van Beuningen, Rotterdam
• *Something About Mary*, The Arnold & Marie Schwartz Gallery Met, New
  York
• *Italics. Italian Art between Tradition and Revolution 1968-2008*, Museum of
  Contemporary Art, Chicago
• *Un certain état du monde? – A selection of works from the François Pinault
  Foundation*, The Garage CCC, Moscow

2008

• *Italics. Italian Art between Tradition and Revolution 1968-2008*, Palazzo
  Grassi, Venezia

- *Review*, Galerie Neu, Berlin
- *Head To Head: Political Portraits*, Museum für Gestaltung, Zürich
- *I Want a Little Sugar in My Bowl*, Asia Song Society, New York
- *The Cinema Effect: Illusion, Reality, and the Moving Image. Part II: Realisms*, Hirshhorn Museum and Sculpture Garden, Washington DC
- *Thoughts on Democracy*, The Wolfsonian FIU, Miami
- *Focus on Contemporary Italian Art*, MAMBO Museo d'Arte Moderna di Bologna, Bologna
- *Martian Museum of Terrestrial Art – Mission: to Interpret and Understand Contemporary Art*, Barbican Centre, London

- *Les fleurs du mal*, Arcos – Museo d'Arte Contemporanea del Sannio, Benevento
- *Senso Unico: A Show of Eight Contemporary Italian Artists*, P.S.1 Contemporary Art Center, New York
- *Passage du Temps: une sélection d'œuvres autour de l'image*, François Pinault Foundation, Tri Postal, Lille
- *Looking Up*, Mário Sequeira Gallery, Braga
- *Vertigo: il secolo di arte off-media dal Futurismo al web*, MAMBO Museo d'Arte Moderna di Bologna, Bologna
- *Apocalittici e integrati: utopia nell'arte italiana di oggi*, MAXXI Museo Nazionale delle Arti del XXI secolo, Roma

- *5th Taipei Biennial*, Taipei Fine Arts Museum, Taipei
- *Highlights from the KunstFilmBiennale Köln in Berlin*, KW Institute for Contemporary Art, Berlin
- *Neo-con: Contemporary Returns to Conceptual Art*, The British School at Rome, Roma
- *6th Shanghai Biennale*, Shanghai Art Museum, Shanghai
- *Neo-con: Contemporary Returns to Conceptual Art*, Apexart, New York
- *À la recherche d'une beauté disparue: omaggio a Luchino Visconti*, GC.AC Galleria Comunale d'Arte Contemporanea, Monfalcone (Gorizia)
- *Yes Bruce Nauman*, Zwirner and Wirth, New York
- *Le Paradoxe du comédien – Figures de l'acteur*, Collection Lambert, Avignon
- *People*, MADRE Museo d'Arte Contemporanea Donna Regina, Napoli
- *Review: Videos from the Pierre Huber Collection*, Magasin – Centre National d'art Contemporain, Grenoble
- *La force de l'art*, Galeries Nationales du Grand Palais, Paris
- *Short History of Performance IV,* Whitechapel Art Gallery, London
- *Message personnel*, Galerie Yvon Lambert, Paris

• *The Adelaide Festival of Arts 2006*, Adelaide
• *The 2006 Whitney Biennial*, Whitney Museum of American Art, New York
• *Satellite of Love*, Witte de With Center for Contemporary Art, Rotterdam
• *Hollywood Boulevard*, Galeria Fortes Vilaça, São Paulo

2005
• *Superstars: Celebrity Factor in Art from Warhol to Madonna*, Kunsthalle
  Wien, Wien
• *Square. Die Sammlung Marli Hoppe-Ritter*, Museum Ritter, Waldenbuch
• *Kunst Film Biennale Köln*, Kölnischer Kunstverein, Köln
• *Omaggio al quadrato*, Galleria Franco Noero, Torino
• *Dall'occhio elettronico. La collezione video del Castello di Rivoli Museo
  d'Arte Contemporanea*, Castello di Rivoli Museo d'Arte Contemporanea,
  Rivoli (Torino)
• *Girls on Film*, Zwirner and Wirth, New York
• *51ª Esposizione Internazionale d'Arte,* La Biennale di Venezia, Venezia
• *Expanded Painting • Prague Biennale 2*, Karlin Hall, Praga
• *Contrabandistas de Imágenes: Selección 26ª Bienal de São Paulo*, Espacio
  Quinta Normal, MAC Museo de Arte Contemporáneo, Santiago de Chile
• *XIV Quadriennale d'arte di Roma,* Palazzo delle Esposizioni, Roma
• *Lo sguardo italiano. Fotografie italiane di moda dal 1951 a oggi*, Rotonda di
  via Besana, Milano
• *African Queen*, The Studio Museum in Harlem, New York
• *BYO. Bring Your Own*, MAN Museo d'Arte Provincia di Nuoro, Nuoro

2004
• *Experiments with Truth*, The Fabric Workshop and Museum, Philadelphia
• *Nuit blanche*, Hôpital Cochin (Port Royal Chapter House), Paris
• *26a Bienal de São Paulo*, Pavilhão da Bienal (Ciccillo Matarazzo), Parque do
  Ibirapuera, São Paulo
• *TEOTHV – Nocturnal Emissions/Nachtelijke uitspattingen*, Groninger
  Museum, Groningen
• AET – *The Future Has a Silver Lining. Genealogies of Glamour*, Migros
  Museum, Zürich
• AET – *The Yugoslav Biennial of Young Artists Vršac 2004*, Konkordija
  Cultural Centre, Vršac, Beograd
• *Angelo Filomeno, Simon Periton, Philip Taaffe, Francesco Vezzoli*, Gorney
  Bravin + Lee, New York
• *Lucio Fontana*, Museum Franz Gertsch, Burgdorf
• *L'Arte in testa*, MACI Museo Arte Contemporanea Isernia, Isernia

2003

- *Progetto Video*, Sala Murat, Bari
- *Fantastic Prophecy*, BAK Basis voor Actuele Kunst; Academiegalerie, Utrecht
- *New space! Group show!*, Galleria Franco Noero, Torino
- *Edinburgh International Film Festival,* Edinburgh College of Art, Edinburgh
- *Carte blanche*, La Fémis, École Nationale Supérieure des Métiers de l'Image
  et du Son, DAP Centre National des Arts Plastiques, Paris
- *Il racconto del filo. Cucito e ricamo nell'arte contemporanea*, MART Museo
  di Arte Moderna e Contemporanea di Trento e Rovereto, Rovereto

2002

- *VideoZone, The 1st International Video-Art Biennial in Israel*, Center for
  Contemporary Art, Tel Aviv
- *Ipotesi di Collezione,* MACRO Museo d'Arte Contemporanea di Roma,
  Roma
- *Second Liverpool Biennial of Contemporary Art*, Tate Liverpool, Liverpool
- *Premio del Golfo – Biennale Europea Arti Visive 2002*, Palazzo dello Sport,
  La Spezia
- *Disturb*, 1st Public School of Hydra, Hydra
- *Verso il Futuro. Identità nell'arte italiana 1990-2002*, Museo del Corso, Roma
- *Opening Show*, Galleria Roma Roma Roma, Roma
- *Ouverture... arte dall'Italia*, GC.AC Galleria Comunale d'Arte
  Contemporanea, Monfalcone (Gorizia)
- *Penetration*, Friedrich Petzel and Marianne Boesky Gallery, New York
- *Melodrama*, Artium, Centro-Museo Vasco de Arte Contemporàneo, Vitoria;
  Palacios de los Condes de Gabia / Centro Jose Guerrero, Granada; MARCO
  Museo de Arte Contemporàneo, Vigo
- *Spring Forward*, Chanel SoHo, New York
- *Campy Vampy Tacky: Leigh Bowery, Brice Dellsperger, Takashi Ito, Michel
  Journiac, Ugo Rondinone, Francesco Vezzoli, Andy Warhol*, La Criée Centre
  d'Art Contemporain, Rennes
- *De Gustibus – Collezione privata Italia*, Palazzo delle Papesse, Centro Arte
  Contemporanea, Siena

2001

- *East Wing Collection No.5*, Courtauld Institute of Art, Somerset House,
  Strand, London
- *A Sense of Wellbeing: Loss, History and Desires*, Bagni Imperiali, Karlovy Vary
- *The 1st Tirana Biennial,* National Gallery of Arts and National Fair Center,
  Tirana
- *Generator 3*, Baluardo di San Regolo – Giardino Botanico, Lucca

- *Haraldur Jónsson, Annika Strom, Francesco Vezzoli,* Contemporary Art
  Centre, Vilnius
- *Squatters*, Fundação Serralves, Porto
- *Boom! Espresso: arte oggi in Italia*, Manifattura Tabacchi, Firenze
- *49ª Esposizione Internazionale d'Arte,* La Biennale di Venezia, Venezia
- *SurFace*, Lunds Konsthall, Lund
- *Bra mot melankoli – Remedy for Melancholy*, Edsvik konst och kultur,
  Sollentuna; Baltic Art Center, Visby
- *Magic and Loss – Contemporary Italian Video*, Pandemonium: The London
  Festival of Moving Image, The LUX Centre, London

2000
- *Migrazioni e multiculturalità,* Premio per la giovane arte italiana 2000,
  Centro per l'Arte Contemporanea, Roma
- *Generator*, Trevi Flash Art Museum, Trevi (Perugia); Galleria Loretta
  Cristofori, Bologna
- *Group Show*, Anthony d'Offay Gallery, London
- *Art and Facts*, Galleria Franco Noero, Torino

1999
- *EXIT*, Chisenhale Gallery, London.
- *Videodrome*, New Museum of Contemporary Art, New York
- *Omaggi e oltraggi*, Claudia Gian Ferrari Arte Contemporanea, Milano
- *6th International Istanbul Biennial*, Dolmabahçe Cultural Centre, Istanbul

1998
- *Fast Forward: Independent Italian Films and Videos*, Brown University,
  Providence
- *La coscienza luccicante*, Palazzo delle Esposizioni, Roma

1997
- *Fatto in Italia / Made in Italy* (Video selection), Centre d'Art Contemporain,
  Genève; Institute of Contemporary Arts, London; The Institute of
  Contemporary Art, Boston.

Enjoy the New Fragrance (Eva Hesse for Greed), 2009
Inkjet on brocade, wool, cotton and metallic embroidery, custom jewelry
180 x 130 x 5 cm
Courtesy Gagosian Gallery
Ph. Matteo Piazza
Gaetano and Barbara Maccaferri collection
Page 17

Enjoy the New Fragrance (Niki de Saint Phalle for Greed), 2009
Inkjet on brocade, wool, cotton and metallic embroidery, custom jewelry
180 x 130 x 5 cm
Courtesy Gagosian Gallery
Ph. Matteo Piazza
Private collection
Page 18

Enjoy the New Fragrance (Leonor Fini for Greed), 2009
Inkjet on brocade, wool, cotton and metallic embroidery, custom jewelry
180 x 130 x 5 cm
Courtesy Gagosian Gallery
Ph. Matteo Piazza
Prada collection
Page 19

Enjoy the New Fragrance (Tamara de Lempicka for Greed), 2009
Inkjet on brocade, wool, cotton and metallic embroidery, custom jewelry
180 x 130 x 5 cm
Courtesy Gagosian Gallery
Ph. Matteo Piazza
Daniel de Hooge collection
Page 20

Enjoy the New Fragrance (Frida Kahlo for Greed), 2009
Inkjet on brocade, wool, cotton and metallic embroidery, custom jewelry
180 x 130 x 5 cm
Courtesy Gagosian Gallery
Ph. Matteo Piazza
Private collection
Page 21

Enjoy the New Fragrance (Sonia Delaunay for Greed), 2009
Inkjet on brocade, wool, cotton and metallic embroidery, custom jewelry
180 x 130 x 5 cm
Courtesy Gagosian Gallery
Ph. Matteo Piazza
Collection of the artist
Page 22

Enjoy the New Fragrance (Louise Nevelson for Greed), 2009
Inkjet on brocade, wool, cotton and metallic embroidery, custom jewelry
180 x 130 x 5 cm
Courtesy Gagosian Gallery
Ph. Matteo Piazza
Private collection
Page 23

Enjoy the New Fragrance (Tina Modotti for Greed), 2009
Inkjet on brocade, wool, cotton and metallic embroidery, custom jewelry
180 x 130 x 5 cm
Courtesy Gagosian Gallery
Ph. Matteo Piazza
Beatrice Bulgari collection
Page 24

Enjoy the New Fragrance (Giorgia O' Keeffe for Greed), 2009
Inkjet on brocade, wool, cotton and metallic embroidery, custom jewelry
180 x 130 x 5 cm
Courtesy Gagosian Gallery
Ph. Matteo Piazza
Angela Missoni collection
Page 25

Enjoy the New Fragrance (Lee Miller for Greed), 2009
Inkjet on brocade, wool, cotton and metallic embroidery, custom jewelry
180 x 130 x 5 cm
Courtesy Gagosian Gallery
Ph. Matteo Piazza
Ernesto Esposito collection
Page 26

Enjoy the New Fragrance (Meret Oppenheim for Greed), 2009
Inkjet on brocade, wool, cotton and metallic embroidery, custom jewelry
180 x 130 x 5 cm
Courtesy Gagosian Gallery
Ph. Matteo Piazza
Gagosian Gallery
Page 27

Greed, A New Fragrance by Francesco Vezzoli, 2009
HD Video, 1 min.
A project by Francesco Vezzoli
Directed by Roman Polanski
Starring Natalie Portman and Michelle Williams
Costumes by: Miuccia Prada
Director of Photography: Pawel Edelman
Artistic Producer: Luca Corbetta
Executive Producer: Max Brun for Hi! Production
Editing: Hervé de Luze
Set Decorator: Anne Seibel
Hair: Odile Gilbert and Johnny Sapong
Make-up: Eileen Kastner-Delago and Stéphanie Kunz
Still Photo: Guy Ferrandis
Pages 46–51 (backstage), 52–59 (video stills)

Greed, The Perfume That Doesn't Exist, 2009
Crystal, paper, ribbon
40 x 27 x 13 cm
Courtesy Gagosian Gallery
Ph. Matteo Piazza
Raphael Castoriano collection
Page 71

Installation at Gagosian Gallery, Rome
Francesco Vezzoli. *Greed, A New Fragrance by Francesco Vezzoli*, installation
at Gagosian Gallery, Rome, 2009. Courtesy Gagosian Gallery. Ph. Matteo
Piazza
Pages 72–73

Installation at La Conservera
Francesco Vezzoli. *Greed, A New Fragrance by Francesco Vezzoli*, installation
at La Conservera, Centro de Arte Contemporáneo, Ceutí, Murcia, 2011. Ph. La
Industrial
Pages 74–77, 79

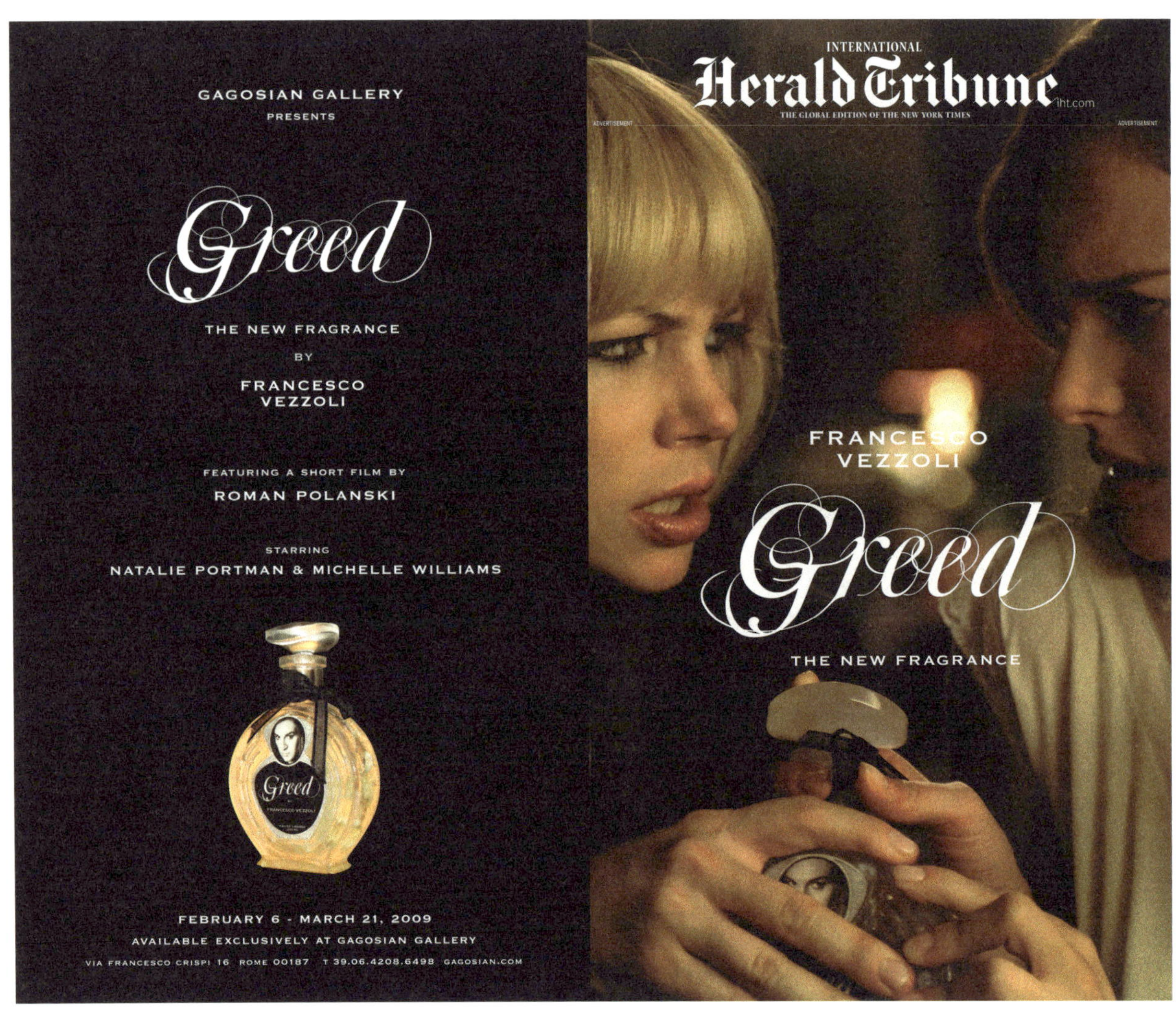

GAGOSIAN GALLERY
PRESENTS

Greed

THE NEW FRAGRANCE
BY
FRANCESCO
VEZZOLI

FEATURING A SHORT FILM BY
ROMAN POLANSKI

STARRING
NATALIE PORTMAN & MICHELLE WILLIAMS

Greed
FRANCESCO VEZZOLI

FEBRUARY 6 - MARCH 21, 2009
AVAILABLE EXCLUSIVELY AT GAGOSIAN GALLERY
VIA FRANCESCO CRISPI 16 ROME 00187 T 39.06.4208.6498 GAGOSIAN.COM

INTERNATIONAL
Herald Tribune
THE GLOBAL EDITION OF THE NEW YORK TIMES
iht.com
ADVERTISEMENT
ADVERTISEMENT

FRANCESCO
VEZZOLI

Greed

THE NEW FRAGRANCE

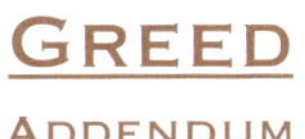

95

On February 6th, 2009, the day of GREED's opening at Gagosian Gallery in Rome, the Italian edition of the *International Herald Tribune* ran a two-page advertising announcing the launch of GREED, "the new fragrance by Francesco Vezzoli."

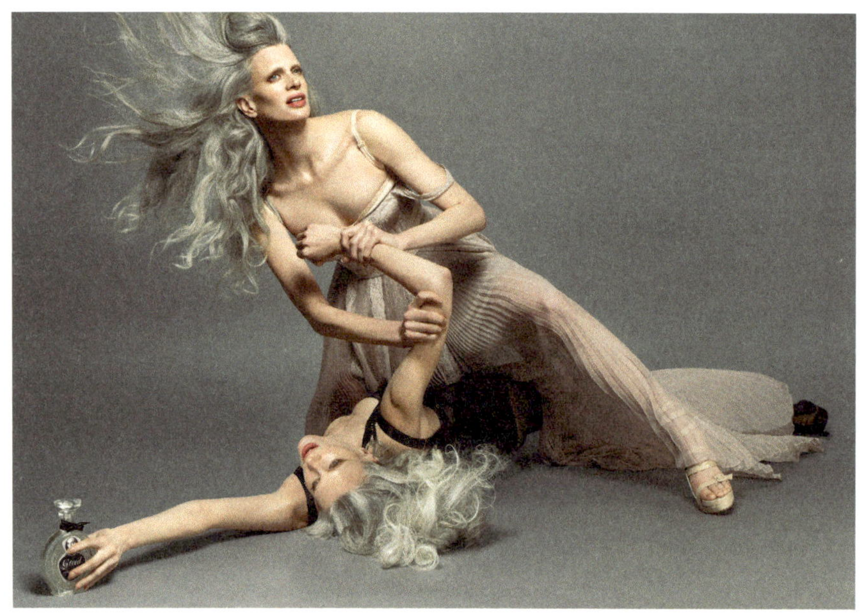

GREED inspired a fashion story photographed by Sølve Sundsbø and featuring the model Kristen McMenamy in a double role. The photos appeared in the March 2009 issue of *V Magazine*.

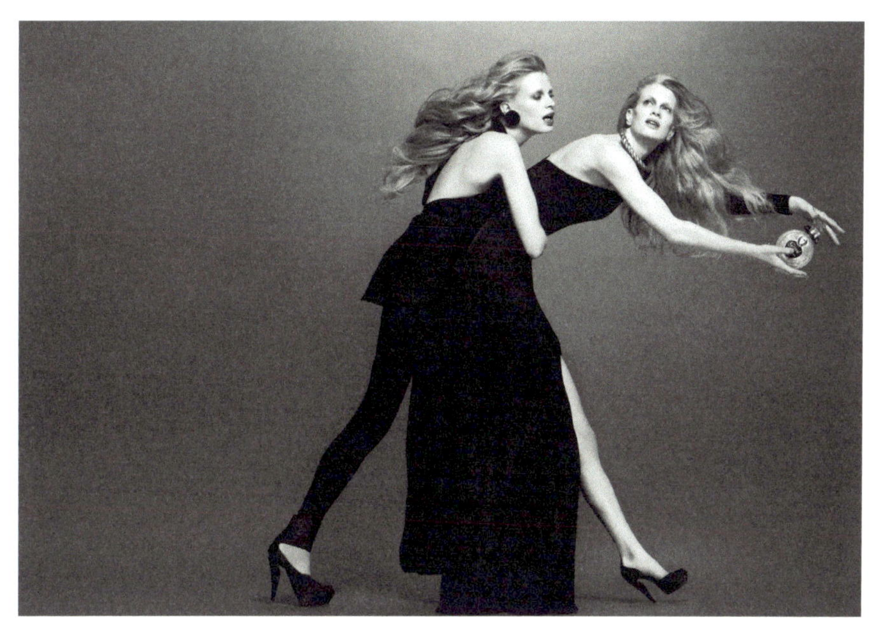

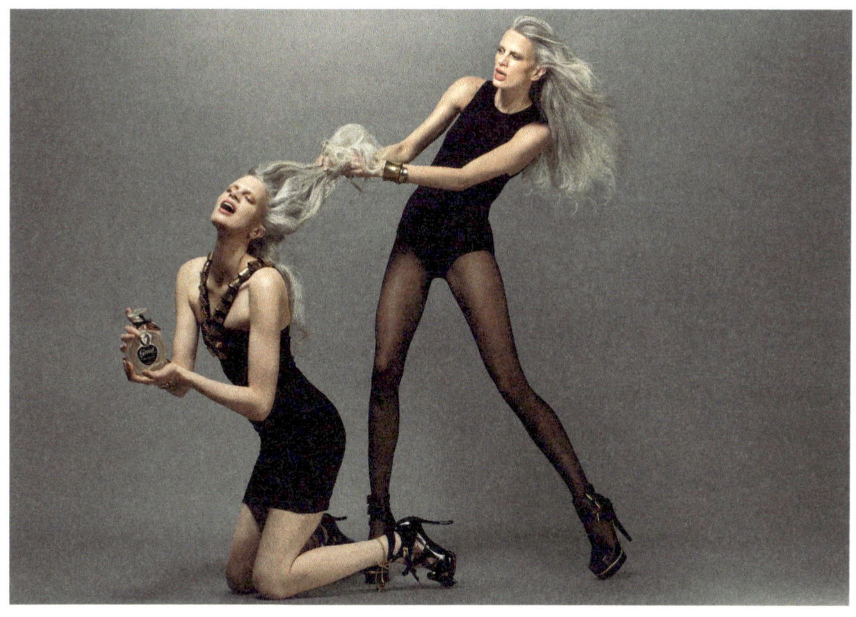

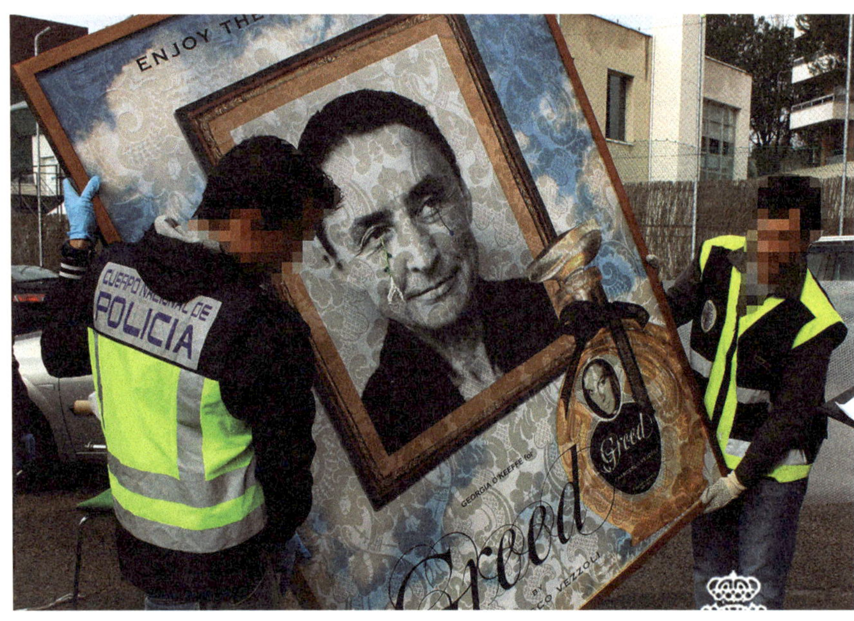

Spanish police agents carrying a piece from Francesco Vezzoli's GREED series. The piece is one of the 35 artworks stolen from a Madrid warehouse on 27 November 2010, from which police has recovered 34, including works by Pablo Picasso, Fernando Botero and Eduardo Chillida.

Francesco Vezzoli wishes to thank:
Herbert Abrell, Christopher Bollen, Max Brun, Felix Burrichter, Valentina Castellani, Nicholas Cullinan, Isabelle Dassonville, Pablo del Val, Bruce Hainley, Antonella Lapetina, Pepi Marchetti Franchi, Cristiana Perrella and Verde Visconti.
Gagosian Gallery and all its crew.
All the team of La Conservera.
The Spanish Police.
Personal thanks to Gioele Amaro.

Francesco Vezzoli expresses his special gratitude to:
Roman Polanski, Natalie Portman, Michelle Williams, Miuccia Prada and Larry Gagosian

La Conservera would like to thank:
The artist.
Beatrice Bulgari, Raphael Castoriano, Daniel de Hooge, Ernesto Esposito, Gaetano and Barbara Maccaferri, Angela Missoni, Miuccia Prada and those who wished to remain anonymous for lending their works to the exhibition.
Cristiana Perrella, Luca Corbetta and Pepi Marchetti Franchi.
Gagosian Gallery and all its crew.

A special gratitude goes to:
Raphael Castoriano, Daniel de Hooge, Gaetano and Barbara Maccaferri, Francesco Vezzoli, Pepi Marchetti Franchi and Cristiana Perrella for their understanding, patience and support during the difficult moments of the surrealist robbery.
The Spanish Police (Grupo XXI de la UDEU de la Brigada Provincial de la Policía Judicial y al Juzgado de Primera Instancia Nº6 de Getafé) for its help and efficiency to solve the surrealist robbery.

COLOPHON

This book was published on the occasion of the exhibition *Greed, A New Fragrance by Francesco Vezzoli*, 3 February - 26 June, 2011, La Conservera, Ceutí (Murcia).

Curator: Cristiana Perrella

Autonomous Community of the Region of Murcia

Ramón Luis Valcárcel Siso
President of the Autonomous Region of Murcia.

Pedro Alberto Cruz Sánchez
Councillor of Culture and Tourism

María Luisa López Ruiz
General Secretary

Juan Antonio Lorca Sánchez
Director-General of Cultural Industries and Arts

La Conservera, Centro de Arte Contemporáneo

Pablo del Val
Director

Pablo Lag
Project Director

María José Santoyo Martín
General Coordinator

María del Carmen Nicolás Navarro
Administration

Isabel Ayala Bañón
Education and Cultural Action

Mercedes García Ibáñez
Press

Exhibition

Installation
Expomed
David José Meseguer Pardo

Insurance
MAPFRE

Transport
Crisóstomo Transportes

La Conservera. Avenida de Lorquí s/n 30562 Ceutí (Murcia) Spain.

Publication

Editor: Cristiana Perrella

Texts: Christopher Bollen, Nicholas Cullinan, Bruce Hainley, Cristiana Perrella, FrancescoVezzoli

Creative Consultant: Felix Burrichter, New York

Photo Credits: La Industrial, Matteo Piazza

Translations: Transit.eu

Graphic design/Typesetting: André Korbmacher, Cologne

Production: Plitt Printmanagement, Oberhausen

Publicado por La Conservera. www.laconservera.org

&

Verlag der Buchhandlung Walther König, Köln
Ehrenstraße 4
50672 Köln
Germany

Tel. +49 (0) 221 / 20 59 6-53
Fax +49 (0) 221 / 20 59 6-60

E-Mail: verlag@buchhandlung-walther-koenig.de

Bibliographic information published by the Deutsche Nationalbibliothek

The Deutsche Nationalbibliothek lists this publication in the Deutsche Nationalbibliografie; detailed bibliographic data are available in the Internet at http://dnb.d-nb.de.

Printed in Germany

Distribution:

Switzerland
Buch 2000
c/o AVA Verlagsauslieferungen AG
Centralweg 16
CH-8910 Affoltern a.A.
Tel. +41 (44) 762 42 00
Fax +41 (44) 762 42 10
E-Mail: a.koll@ava.ch

UK & Eire
Cornerhouse Publications
70 Oxford Street
GB-Manchester M1 5NH
Fon +44 (0) 161 200 15 03
Fax +44 (0) 161 200 15 04
E-Mail: publications@cornerhouse.org

Outside Europe
D.A.P. / Distributed Art Publishers, Inc.
155 6th Avenue, 2nd Floor
USA-New York, NY 10013
Fon +1 212 627 1999
Fax +1 212 627 9484

www.artbook.com

ISBN 978-3-86560-949-6